SOPHIA IN EXILE

Die Philosophische Kugel oder das Wunder-Auge der Ewigkeit.

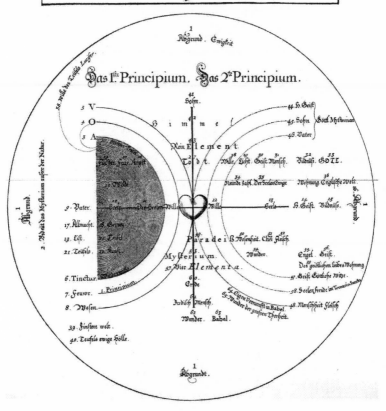

Sophia
in Exile

MICHAEL MARTIN

Angelico Press

First published in the USA
by Angelico Press 2021
Copyright © Michael Martin 2021

For information, address:
Angelico Press, Ltd.
169 Monitor St.
Brooklyn, NY 11222
www.angelicopress.com

paper 978-1-62138-778-7
cloth 978-1-62138-779-4

Book and cover design
by Michael Schrauzer

for Bonnie

"I will go to the mountain of myrrh
and to the hill of incense."

CONTENTS

INTRODUCTION
Notes from Exile

AFTER FRANCIS OF ASSISI AND HIS COMpanions walked the hundred and ten or so miles from Assisi to Rome, a trek that took days, in order to petition approval for founding the Order of Friars Minor, the cardinals interviewing them asked what their rule would be. Pretty straightforward question. Francis, a pretty straightforward man, held up the book of the Gospels. The cardinalate thought he must be either mistaken or a fool, since such a rule "seemed a thing untried, and too hard for human strength."[1] That says pretty much all we need to know about ecclesial governance. Very few princes of the Church take out their own garbage or dirty their hands with manual labor. Living close to the Gospel, for all their preaching, is ultimately impractical: at worst a nuisance, at best an ideal. Even the order Francis founded couldn't live up to its own principles and strayed from them during Francis's lifetime. It brought him great sorrow.

When it happened, I had no idea how prophetic an event the tragic fire at Notre-Dame de Paris on 15 April 2019 would prove to be. It's a fitting icon for a Church in distress, suffering from the weight of its own corruption, not least the ongoing sex scandals that fill us with shame and anger, evidence as they are of an ecclesial structure inured to the sufferings of its victims, and further complicated by the manner in which some of its most powerful leaders have continued to shield their own from scrutiny. These are symptoms of a deeper pathology. The hierarchy's inept and milquetoasty response to the global pandemic that began in early 2020 only further betrays how

---

1 Bonaventura, *The Life of Saint Francis of Assisi* (London: J. M. Dent, 1904), 30.

indifference has become a cardinal virtue. How many millions died without receiving the last sacraments? How many more left the Church permanently because it was too hard for the hierarchy to live out the Gospel and too easy to play the political sycophant? Did Christ wait until lepers were no longer contagious to heal them?

It was under these conditions and in this frame of mind that I wrote this book.

This book, however, is not a jeremiad on the sins and ineptitude of the hierarchy, or even about living through the madness of the pandemic. These things, I think, are only tangential, though nonetheless symptomatic, of a deeper estrangement from the Real that is the true source of our cosmological dissociation, and which has its roots deep in the historical Christian imaginary. This dissociation did not begin with the conflagration of Notre-Dame, nor with the complicity of bishops in the abuses among their ranks. When Christ told Francis "Rebuild my Church," he was not speaking of San Damiano, though that was what Francis thought at the time. Perhaps he was telling us the same thing with the burning of Notre-Dame, for "every man's work shall be made manifest: for the day shall declare it, because it shall be revealed by fire" (1 Cor 3:13).

I began this book in late 2019 when I wrote the first chapter, after which the book is named. I did not return to the project until fall of 2020, the confusion of the pandemic and work on my farm taking all of my attention in the interim. Looking at it now, the book can be called the third in a trilogy that started with *The Submerged Reality* (2015) and continued with *Transfiguration* (2018), though writing a trilogy was at no point my intention. But here we are. I felt the need to write this book because I came to realize that I had left some things, such as the Gnostic mythos of Sophia and the sophiological structure of marriage, undeveloped in those previous books, and I wanted to provide insight into the poetic metaphysics of Sophiology by deeper examinations of Eleanor Farjeon, Thomas Traherne, the legend of the Holy Grail, the Rosary, and the radical Christian philosophy of Nikolai Berdyaev (the chapter on whom was originally published in the Russian journal тетради по консерватизму [*Essays on Conservatism*]). In addition, I felt a call to write on the Creation and our relationship to it — as a biodynamic farmer, this is an environment in which I live and move and have my being — as well as to contribute something on the role of human creativity. These areas of contemplation organically brought me to a consideration of the Realm of Faerie, which has thankfully been getting more serious attention from John Milbank and David Bentley Hart, among others.

As a result of all these commitments and interests, what you have in your hands here is (with the exception of my poetry) the most personal of all of my books to this point. Sophiology, it is my contention, is above all something one *does*, a way of being. It is not a grand theory, a beautiful intellectual construction. No. Sophiology is an entrance into life.

In the Gnostic mythos, Sophia lives in exile, trapped in a kind of spiritual prison. We, too, live in exile, which is also a spiritual prison. Most of all, we live in exile from the Divine and the Creation. As the pandemic and the ever-increasing totalization of the technocracy have shown, we are also in exile from each other, and, ultimately, from ourselves. This is an untenable situation and one which, if left unchecked, will have disastrous repercussions, many of which are deep into their implementation stages. The antidote to such a situation, as I argue in these pages, lies in reorienting ourselves to the Real, to the sophianic structure of the world. As with St. Francis's project, this is one of simplicity and not applicable to the needs of hierarchies of power and influence. In essence, what Sophiology offers is a regeneration of life by an engagement with what is Real. And this regeneration is conditioned by learning how to see.

Love is integral to this seeing, as both agapeic opening and as erotic longing. This integral seeing in not characterized by a spiritual acquisitiveness or desire to possess, so much as it is a product of the subject's entrance into a loving disposition to that which shines through the world. St. Paul describes such a condition in 1 Corinthians: "If anyone imagines that he knows something, he does not yet know as he ought to know. But if anyone loves God, he is known by God" (8:2-3). Those who try to turn Sophiology (or any theological or philosophical gesture) into a method for comprehending or containing the world are barking up the wrong sacred tree. The first movement is in love, and the response to love is not "to know" but to be known.

And in that spirit, I welcome you to these pages.

I

Sophia in Exile

Who has gone up into heaven, and taken her, and
brought her down from the clouds?

~:Baruch 3:29

But where is wisdom to be found?

~:Job 28:20

FORGETFULNESS. IT ALL BEGINS WITH
forgetfulness.

The Gnostic mythos in general, and the story of
Sophia's fall and reascent in particular, is a mythos of forgetfulness, a mythos of spiritual amnesia on a divine scale. Forgetfulness, in the Gnostic imaginary, becomes the vessel (which is
not a vessel) of exile. Exile, then, is not a punishment imposed
from without, but an ontological state, a dislocation of being.
The beauty (which is tragedy) of this condition resides in the
fact that forgetfulness obscures, erases from being the awareness
of the actual nature of its reality, from the Real. Certainly, such
an imaginary bears resemblance to the Hindu notion that all
we perceive is nothing but *maya*, illusion. But the sickness of
forgetfulness is not without cure. Remembering, the recollec-
tion of self, is the cure, which, in Plato's concept of *anamnesis*,
is literally an "unforgetting."

The Gnostic Hymn of the Pearl (also known as The Hymn
of the Robe of Glory), appended to some manuscripts of The
Gospel of Thomas, in fairy-tale-like manner relates the story
of a king's son sent to the Land of Egypt to retrieve a pearl
in possession of a serpent. But when the young man arrives,
he makes acquaintance with those who distract him from

his mission and offer him their food and drink. Once he has taken of their refreshment (a true anti-eucharist), a shroud of oblivion covers him:

> I forgot that I was a King's son,
> And became a slave to their king.
> I forgot all concerning the Pearl
> For which my Parents had sent me;
> And from the weight of their victuals
> I sank down into a deep sleep.[1]

In the greater Gnostic mythos, Sophia, momentarily forgetting who she is, desires to imitate the Father's divine creativity and inadvertently gives birth to an abomination, Yaldabaoth. Sophia withdraws as a result of her presumption, and Yaldabaoth, not knowing his own origin, believes himself to be the Creator God.[2] He doesn't know who or what he is; though, like all of us, he is certain he does. Ignorant of his own nature, Yaldabaoth builds a false world, a world characterized by wickedness and dissemblance. He wields, we might say, supreme executive power. Or so he thinks.

In the absence of the Real, simulacra of the Real fill the void, a situation described in 1 Enoch:

> Wisdom could not find a place in which she could dwell;
> but a place was found in the heavens.
> Then Wisdom went out to dwell with the children of
> the people,
> but she found no dwelling place.
> Wisdom returned to her place
> and she settled permanently among the angels.
> Then Iniquity went out of her rooms,
> and found whom she did not expect.
> And she dwelt with them,

---

1 G. R. S. Mead, trans. and ed., *Echoes from the Gnosis, Vol X: The Hymn of the Robe of Glory* (London: Theosophical Publishing Company, 1908), lines 33–35.
2 For example, in the Nag Hammadi documents, *The Apocryphon of John* and *On the Origin of the World*.

like rain in a desert,
like dew on a thirsty land. (42:1–3)[3]

Nature abhors a vacuum. If it cannot be filled with the Good,
it will be filled with something else. Politics, art, science, community, religion: all these belong to Nature, for they are of the
human, and all suffer from an emptiness filled by the demiurgic
simulacra of creation.

Nature responds to — resounds with — consciousness, as
even the most rudimentary experiences with intentionality
disclose. The reality of what David Bohm called "implicate
order" is something children intuitively realize, something
Thomas Traherne, for instance, returns to again and again in
his poetic reverie. "Nature," that is, "is naturally intoxicated
with consciousness and consciousness is purposeless without
nature."[4] We are implicit in the cosmos, and the cosmos is
implicit in us. This reality, apparent in the synergy between
the microcosm and the macrocosm, was a foundational intuition in Western thinking through the early modern period,
before modernity hid it in the attic of Western civilization as
a primitive embarrassment, like a high school yearbook with
its panoply of bad haircuts. Ignored or not, its reality is evident all around us. Cut off from the cosmos, the microcosm
is disordered, sick, unable to realize itself. Likewise does the
macrocosm become disordered and likewise is it profoundly
unable to realize itself. To deny this is to deny the Real. Truly,
all the foundations of the earth are out of course.

It is precisely this distorted relationship to the Real that the
myriad permutations of the Gnostic mythos explore. Some
may scoff at the Gnostic view of the universe as a place hostile

3 James H. Charlesworth, ed. The Old Testament Pseudepigrapha, Volume One:
Apocalyptic Literature and Testaments (New York: Doubleday & Company, 1983).
4 A. K. Mukhopadhyay, "The Self and Its Memes and Genes: Genes, Memes,
Self, Brain, Information and Consciousness," in History of Science, Philosophy
and Culture in Indian Civilization, Volume XIII Part 6: History of Science and
Philosophy of Science: A Historical Perspective of the Evolution of ideas in Science,
ed. Pradip Kumar Sengupta (New Delhi: Longman, 2010), 481–558, at 505.

to the Good, at the story of Sophia's fall and her diabolical progeny Yaldabaoth, at the notion of wicked Archons manipulating reality to their liking — but take a look at the history of politics, religion, science, and art, at the decrepitude that has been inflicted upon the environment, and we discover that maybe the Gnostics weren't so deluded after all. Perception creates our reality: if we have faulty organs of perception, we create a faulty reality (which is far from the Real). How we see creates *what* we see, and we become what we see. As Blake so succinctly phrases it, "They became what they beheld." [5]

The Gnostic mythos, it has to be admitted, is nothing if not pessimistic: indeed, nihilistic. The Gnostics saw the only possibility for salvation as escape from a thoroughly corrupted universe through knowledge (*gnosis*). They recognized the absurdity of human life, and though their mythos is charged with imaginative wonder, their conclusion about our state is no less brutal and disturbing. As Hans Jonas contemplates at the end of his early magisterial study of Gnosticism, the Gnostics present us with evidence of our metaphysical disrupture:

> The disruption between man and total reality is at the bottom of nihilism. The illogicality of the rupture, that is, of a dualism without metaphysics, makes its fact no less real, nor its seeming alternative any more acceptable: the stare at isolated selfhood, to which it condemns man, may wish to exchange itself for a monistic naturalism which, along with the rupture, would abolish also the idea of man as man. Between that Scylla and this her twin Charybdis, the modern mind hovers. Whether a third road is open to it — one by which the dualistic rift can be avoided and yet enough of the dualistic insight saved to uphold the humanity of man — philosophy must find out. [6]

5 William Blake, *Jerusalem, the Emanation of the Giant Albion*, ed. Morton D. Paley (Princeton: Princeton University Press, 1994), plate 36 [32], page 186.
6 Hans Jonas, *The Gnostic Religion: The Message of the Alien God and the Beginnings of Christianity*, 2nd ed. (Boston: Beacon Press, 1963), 340.

Sophiology, as I will continue to argue, offers the only alternative to both Gnostic pessimism (whether religious or secular) and the fanciful idealism infecting so many religious traditions (Christianity no less than Hinduism) that the earth is not our real home and that our ultimate destination resides in an amorphous "elsewhere": an elsewhere identical with the Derridean Messiah — the Messiah who never arrives.

SOPHIA IN THE KABBALAH: THE SHEKINAH

Echoing in many ways the exile of Sophia in Gnosticism, the figure of the Shekinah found in the Kabbalah nonetheless offers a slightly different perspective on the presence of the Divine Feminine both in the world and in human interiority, in ontology as well as teleology.

Whether or not the Shekinah was or was not considered a Divine Person before the medieval period is the subject of debate. Indeed, the term "Shekinah" does not appear in the Hebrew Bible, though it does show up in the Talmud where it denotes "God's dwelling place," his presence in the world, or tabernacle. *Hokmah*, or Wisdom (Sophia), however, does appear in the biblical literature, though Gershom Scholem, reading Proverbs 8, does not see any evidence that Sophia is depicted as anything other than a "craftsman" and certainly not an aspect of YHWH, let alone God's spouse.[7] Others disagree. Moshe Idel, for example, Scholem's protégé and heir as elder statesman on the Kabbalah, reads the Sophia of Proverbs as a divine female, even a *hypostasis*.[8] Moshe Weinfeld, while acknowledging that the word "Shekinah" does not appear in the Hebrew Bible, does note its presence in the New Testament, pointing to Revelation 21:3: "Behold the σκηνὴ [*skēnē*,

---

7 Gershom Scholem, *On the Mystical Shape of the Godhead*, trans. Joachim Neugroschel, ed. and rev. Jonathan Chipman (New York: Schocken Books, 1991), 142.
8 Moshe Idel, *The Privileged Divine Feminine in Kabbalah* (Berlin: De Gruyter, 2019), 6.

here read as a Greek transliteration of *Shekinah*, rather than translated as 'tabernacle'] is with mankind, it will dwell with them."[9] Context is even more important than etymology, as these words are preceded by the description of "the Holy City, the new Jerusalem, coming down out of heaven from God, prepared as a bride beautifully dressed for her husband" (21:2). But I'm not interested in historicity as such. I'm interested in truth, and the truth is that over the course of time Hokmah/Sophia was conflated with the Shekinah. Arthur Green has called this development "the unequivocal feminization of *shekhinah* in the Kabbalah of the thirteenth century, a Jewish response to, and adaptation of, the revival of devotion to Mary in the twelfth century Western church."[10] To interpret this development as mere cultural cross-pollination, however, is to miss the point. My concern here is the "fugitive truth" of Sophia as revealed *in* time and *over* time, of the irruption of Sophia into human awareness, an awakening to the sophianic always/already present, just as the laws of mathematics were always/already present in the universe but only awaited the arrival of intellects capable of disclosing and articulating them.

As with Sophia in Gnosticism, the Shekinah of the Kabbalah is often spoken of in terms of exile: an image echoing the tragic exiles of the Jews from the land of Israel and the soul's apparent exile from God. Shekinah's exile, furthermore, represents a kind of forgetfulness, the forgetfulness of sleep, as found in the *Tiqqune haZohar*: "wake up from your sleep, wake up and sing to awaken the Shekhina for she is asleep in the Exile."[11] Unlike the Gnostic Sophia, the Shekinah's exile resulted not

---

9   Moshe Weinfeld, "Feminine Features in the Imagery of God in Israel: The Sacred Marriage and the Sacred Tree," *Vetus Testamentum*, 46, no. 4 (1996): 515–29, at 521. Weinfeld's contextualization.

10   Arthur Green, "Shekhinah, the Virgin Mary, and the Song of Songs: Reflections on a Kabbalistic Symbol in Its Historical Context," *Association of Jewish Studies*, 26, no. 1 (Apr 2002): 1–52, at 1.

11   Quoted in Raphael Patai, *The Hebrew Goddess*, 3rd ed. (Detroit: Wayne State University Press, 1990), 164.

from her own supernatural transgressions, but from the sinful actions of the Hebrew people (certainly the *leitmotif* of the Hebrew Bible). As a result, "the privileged status is to be sought in the eyes of the Kabbalist, who focuses his religious life on helping her."[12] The Shekinah's reunion with the Holy One, then, figures the promised redemption of Israel, which is why Kabbalists have followed every pious act with the formula "for the sake of the reunion of God and His *Shekinah.*"[13] Likewise echoing the Gnostic mythos, Lurianic Kabbalah also speaks of "the sparks" of the Shekinah scattered throughout Creation, a thoroughly exilic figure. In the Kabbalah such sparks are also the consequence of the breaking of the vessels, and this certainly suggests that the Tree of Life is synonymous with the Shekinah, a connection made by Moshe Weinfeld among others.[14] The Zohar, in its beautifully imaginative idiom, describes this condition symbolically:

> What is a beautiful maiden who has no eyes
> and a body concealed and revealed?
> She comes out in the morning and is hidden all day.
> She adorns herself with adornments that are not.[15]

For the always circumspect Scholem, the idea of sparks of the Shekinah represents a "dissolving" of the concept of Shekinah as feminine divine person.[16] Seeing the impact the idea of the Divine Feminine of the Kabbalah had on Behmenist thought and Sophiology over the five centuries following the Reformation, it may be that his scholarly apparatus, colored by myths of progress and logical positivism, became a hindrance to his powers of perception.

---

12 Moshe Idel, *The Privileged Divine Feminine in Kabbalah*, 81.

13 Gershom Scholem, *On the Kabbalah and Its Symbolism*, trans. Ralph Manheim (London: Routledge & Kegan Paul, 1965), 108.

14 Moshe Weinfeld, "Feminine Features in the Imagery of God in Israel," 515–17.

15 *Zohar: The Book of Enlightenment*, trans. Daniel Chanan Matt (New York: Paulist Press, 1983), 121.

16 Gershom Scholem, *On the Mystical Shape of the Godhead*, 193.

Perhaps the most important resonance between the Gnostic and Kabbalistic systems can be found in the paradigm of emergence, descent, and reascent of Sophia and the Shekinah. Idel identifies this progression itself as uroboric, drawing on the pseudo-Aristotelian dictum "the first in thought is the last in action," which he argues was integral to late-medieval kabbalistic theosophy.[17] In this paradigm as adopted by the kabbalists, "the final cause, considered as the highest of the four causes in Aristotelian terminology [along with material, formal, and efficient causes], occurs first in thought, although its implementation in action . . . occurs later. According to this mode of thought, later may even be better." Explaining further, he diagrams this movement in what he calls "the three phases gender model": "the emergence of the divine Feminine from a very elevated entity in the theosophical systems; Her descent — or more rarely fall; and Her return to the initial place in privileged moments, such as the Sabbath and in the eschaton."[18] On the kabbalistic Tree of Life, this implies that Shekinah, usually associated with Malkhut, the lowest of the sephiroth, actually originates in Kether, the highest.

In Gnosticism, Sophia is the last created of the Aeons. The implication that she was first in thought, however, is not at all as apparent in the Gnostic mythos as it is with the Shekinah in kabbalistic theosophy, though the presence of a "lower Sophia" and a "higher Sophia" in some Gnostic schemas (for example, in the *Gospel of Philip*) certainly invites such speculation. Sophia's Fall obviously is foregrounded in the Gnostic mythos; though, whenever parsing mythologies, it is always better to reside in an attitude of conceptual fluidity and not become unnecessarily or dogmatically rigid. Nevertheless, the *Gospel of Thomas* gives credence to the pseudo-Aristotelian dictum: "Jesus said, 'Have you discovered the beginning, then, so that you are seeking the end? For where the beginning is the end will be. Blessed is he

---

17 Moshe Idel, *The Privileged Divine Feminine in Kabbalah*, 21.
18 Ibid., 19.

who stands at the beginning; that one will know the end and will not taste death."[19] This model also shines through the Christian Bible. Reading Proverbs 8, with Wisdom's presence at the Creation — "The Lord brought me forth as the first of his works, before his deeds of old" (22) — as emergence, we can then turn to Revelation's Woman Clothed with the Sun and the New Jerusalem, "adorned as a bride for her bridegroom" as permutations of Sophia's reascent. Likewise, to admittedly stretch the comparison, we can read the progression from Eve's emergence and Fall to the Incarnation of the Virgin as tracing the trajectory from descent to exile to reascent (to say nothing of the Catholic dogmas of the Immaculate Conception and the Assumption of Mary as images of reascent and exaltation). In describing the uroboric movement of the Shekinah in kabbalistic theosophy, Idel limns its resemblances with its Christian counterpart:

> The preeminence of the Female, *Malkhut*, is evident, both in the primordial past and the eschatological future, when She is depicted as even transcending the light of the Sun, namely the Male, as Her Husband. Her description in the eschaton as higher than the sun is indicative of the *imaginaire* or Her grandeur.[20]

Or, in other words:

> A great sign appeared in heaven: a woman clothed with the sun, with the moon under her feet and a crown of twelve stars on her head. (Rev 12:1)

> I saw the Holy City, the new Jerusalem, coming down out of heaven from God, prepared as a bride beautifully dressed for her husband. And I heard a loud voice from the throne saying, "Look! God's dwelling place [Shekinah] is now among the people, and he will dwell with them. They will be his people, and God himself will be with them and be their God." (Rev 21:2–3)

---

19 Thomas 18. *The Nag Hammadi Scriptures.*
20 Ibid., 107.

THE EGYPTIAN EXILE

The notion of exile does not only apply to Sophia in the Judaism of late antiquity, but it also locates the faithful, and the faithful Jews in exile in Alexandria in particular. As the Septuagint reading of Baruch has it: "See, today we are in exile, where you have scattered us, an object of reproach and cursing and punishment for all the wicked deeds of our ancestors, who withdrew from the LORD, our God" (3:8). The Greek here translated as "you have scattered us" (διέσπειρας, *diespeiras*, "diaspora") describes exactly the condition of the Jewish community living in Alexandria from at least the third century BCE. Margaret Barker has argued that the Jewish community living in the diaspora in Egypt also maintained a devotion to Sophia that had been a part of worship in Jerusalem prior to the reforms of Josiah. She suggests that the community in Alexandria persisted in that devotion and, further, that their exile was self-imposed as a way to preserve it. If she's correct — and I think she is — the fact that the Jewish scriptures which arose out of the diasporic community (the books of Sirach and Wisdom, for example) feature Sophia as a central figure should come as no surprise. [21]

In her scholarly excavations, Barker asserts that Wisdom was mistranslated or edited out, if not entirely expunged, from the Hebrew canon of scripture. The Wisdom books, most of them written in Greek, were excluded from the Hebrew canon, which was probably not fixed until the second century CE, if not later. Barker rejects the usual and tired excuse that the Greek language was the reason for the exclusion of the so-called Apocrypha and likewise dismisses the charge that Egyptian Judaism was guilty of the sin of syncretism and imported aspects of Isis or the Great Mother into its religion. [22] For Barker, the diminishment of Sophia from both scripture and worship was programmatic

---

21 Margaret Barker, *The Lady in the Temple*, Vol 1, 231–32.
22 Margaret Barker, *Creation: A Biblical Vision for the Environment* (London: T&T Clark, 2010), 240.

and proceeded by degrees. [23] She reads a lament of Wisdom's expulsion (and the reciprocal expulsion of authentic worship) in Enoch: "All who lived in the temple lost their vision, and the hearts of all of them godlessly forsook Wisdom, and the house of the kingdom was burned and the whole chosen people scattered" (1 Enoch 93.8). [24] The destruction of the temple, that is, was a result of abandoning Sophia. [25] As it is explained in the *Zohar*, "Israel is dead for the Shekinah which is above by the destruction of the First Temple; it is dead a second time by the destruction of the Second Temple." [26] In a curious observation, Barker also reads Miriam's leprosy and expulsion in Numbers 12 as a symbol for the banishment of the Divine Feminine from First Temple Judaism, to which we shall return. [27]

Sophia was similarly exiled from Christianity (though she kept smuggling herself back in) through the ways by which she was unsexed in much Patristic literature (certainly an anxiety provoked by theological debates with Gnosticism) and mysteriously (and sloppily) conflated with the Logos. Furthermore, as Paul Evdokimov has observed, "At one time, serious theologians discussed whether or not woman had a soul," so we should not act with any indignation at the suggestion that at least some of the Fathers lacked an appreciation for the Divine Feminine, or for anything feminine for that matter. [28] This anx-

---

23 Ibid., 243–45.
24 Another translation: ". . . those who happen to be in it [the Temple] shall all of them be blindfolded, and the hearts of them all shall forget wisdom. And, at its completion, the house of the kingdom shall be burnt with fire; and therein the whole clan of the chosen root shall be dispersed." James H. Charlesworth, ed. *The Old Testament Pseudepigrapha*, Volume 1: *Apocalyptic Literature and Testaments* (Garden City, NY: Doubleday & Company, 1983).
25 Margaret Barker, *Temple Theology: An Introduction* (London: SPCK, 2004), 75.
26 pt I, fol, 26a. Quoted in Arthur Edward Waite, *The Secret Doctrine in Israel: A Study of the Zohar and Its Connections* (London: Rebman, 1911), 211.
27 Margaret Barker, *The Mother of the Lord*, Volume I: *The Lady in the Temple* (London: Bloomsbury, 2012), 67.
28 Paul Evdokimov, *Woman and the Salvation of the World: A Christian Anthropology on the Charisms of Women*, trans. Anthony P. Gythiel (Crestwood,

iety was fortified by the anxiety about sex the Fathers inherited from Platonism and Neoplatonism — and not Judaism — and imported into monasticism. Again, from Evdokimov:

> Certain forms of asceticism that prescribe avoiding one's mother, and even animals of the female sex, say a great deal about the loss of psychic balance. The loss explains the opinions about married love held by certain Doctors of the Church — opinions drawn, it seems, from manuals of zoology, whereby the couple is viewed from the perspective of breeding.[29]

John Paul II's Theology of the Body certainly tried to remedy this situation, but it was, really, too little, too late — two thousand years too late. As recent history has only too painfully made us aware, the time has come for a more robust reclamation of a holistically Christian attitude towards sex and wrest it from the hotbeds of neurosis and pathology that so pollute Christian power structures.

ECHOES FROM THE GNOSIS

On Christmas Eve and Christmas Day of 1920 philosopher, esotericist, and cultural reformer Rudolf Steiner gave a pair of lectures at the Goetheanum, the architectural marvel he built in Dornach, Switzerland as the headquarters of the Anthroposophical Society. The title of the lectures was "The Search for the New Isis," and in them Steiner grapples with the problems individuals face when trying to inculcate an authentic Christianity into their lives. Steiner was very concerned about the technological and materialistic thinking that permeated (and continues to permeate) Western culture. In the lectures he works with the story of Isis-as-Sophia and connects the Egyptian mythos to Christianity. This may seem a stretch, but any Christian who has ever read Apuleius's account of the

---

NY: St. Vladimir's Seminary Press, 1994), 243.
29 Ibid., 27.

theophany of Isis could not fail to recognize its family resemblance to Marian apparitions. As Apuleius's protagonist Lucius describes her in *The Golden Ass*:

> She wore a multi-colored gown, woven of the finest linen, part gleaming white, part crocus yellow, and part flaming rose-red. But what left me staring was the deep jet-black of her mantle, slung across her body from the right hip to the left shoulder, where it was knotted in something like the boss of a shield and then hung down in a series of folds to its tasseled fringes. It was embroidered all over with glittering stars and in the middle a moon shone like flames of fire. A beautiful garland of flowers and fruits ran along the edges of this garment.[30]

One ingredient of Steiner's antidote to the technological materialism of the age consists in our simply becoming cognizant of the fact that, in Gerard Manley Hopkin's apt phrase, "the world is charged with the grandeur of God." In richly imaginative language, Steiner describes how we might think of such a reality:

> We must realize that through the force of the Christ we must find an inner astronomy that will show us again the cosmos moving and working by the power of the spirit. When we have this insight into the cosmos that is awakened through the newfound Isis power of the Christ — which is now the power of the Divine Sophia — then Christ, united with the Earth since the Mystery of Golgotha, will become active within us, because we shall know him. It is not the Christ that we lack, but the knowledge and wisdom of Isis, the Sophia of the Christ.[31]

Steiner, however, does not necessarily lament the lost connection to the spiritual in the world and to the Divine which has

---

30 "The Vision of Isis" from *The Golden Ass* by Apuleius, trans. Elias Crim in *Jesus the Imagination, Volume II: The Being of Marriage* (Kettering, OH: Angelico Press, 2018): 56–59, at 57.
31 Rudolf Steiner, *Isis Mary Sophia: Her Mission and Ours: Selected Lectures and Writings*, ed. Christopher Bamford (Herndon, VA: Steiner Books, 2003), 211.

been part and parcel of modernity. For him, this is all part of a spiritual-evolutionary process that will, in the end, allow people to come to a more mature faith, a faith based on immediate knowledge of the Divine in both the natural and supernatural spheres. Steiner sees Paul's words in 1 Corinthians as mystical-evolutionary fact: "When I was a child, I spoke as a child, I understood as a child, I thought as a child; but when I became a man, I put away childish things" (13:11). Whether or not one agrees with him, he certainly lends more optimism (and less finality) when faced with the totalizing effects of the techno-cratic cosmos in which we now suffer. Steiner's contemporary Nikolai Berdyaev came to a similar insight, though perhaps one more pessimistic in the short run, when he wrote that "either a new epoch in Christianity is in store for us and a Christian renaissance will take place, or Christianity is doomed to per-ish," though he knew full well that the gates of hell would not prevail against it.[32]

Steiner closes the first lecture with a verse depicting the esoteric ideas he puts forth. It draws on Gnostic and Classical Egyptian as well as Christian motifs:

> Isis-Sophia
> Wisdom of God
> Lucifer has slain her,
> And on wings of cosmic forces
> Carried her away into the depths of space.
> Christ-Will
> Working in us
> Shall tear her from Lucifer
> And on grounds of spiritual knowledge
> Call to new life in human souls
> Isis-Sophia
> Wisdom of God.[33]

---

32 Nikolai Berdyaev, *Freedom and the Spirit*, trans. Oliver Fielding Clarke (London: Geoffrey Bles/The Centenary Press, 1935), 46.
33 Rudolf Steiner, *Isis Mary Sophia*, 214.

Steiner's appropriation of the Gnostic exile/captivity mythos of Sophia is purposeful, and he explains it in terms of the diminishment of the Virgin Mary's importance in Christianity:

> Christ will appear in spiritual form during the twentieth century not simply because something happens outwardly, but to the extent that we find the power represented by holy Sophia. Our time tends to lose this Isis-power, this power of the Mary. It was killed by all that arose with the modern consciousness of humankind. *New forms of religion have, in part, killed just this view of Mary.*[34]

As we have seen from the trajectory traced by Barker and illustrated through Gnosticism and kabbalistic theosophy (and without mentioning the reduced role of Mary in Protestant and, let's face it, some modern Catholic and Orthodox theologies), Steiner definitely has a case.

In the aftermath of World War II, erstwhile follower of Steiner, the Catholic hermeticist Valentin Tomberg was living with his wife and young son in a camp for displaced persons in the Netherlands when he met Ida Peerdeman, the visionary of the Marian apparition known as the Lady of All Nations. Around that time, he contributed a curious prayer that also evokes the Sophia exile motif in sacred parody of the *Pater Noster*:

> Our Mother,
> Thou who art in the darkness of the underworld,
> May the holiness of thy name shine a light anew on our remembering,
> May the breath of thy awakening kingdom warm all who wander homeless.
> May the resurrection of thy will renew eternal faithfulness even to the depths of physical substance.
> Receive today the living remembrance of thee from human hearts,
> Who implore you to forgive the sin of forgetting thee,
> And are ready to fight against the temptation

---

34   Ibid., 213–14. My emphasis.

That has led you to existence in the darkness,
That through the deed of the Son, the immeasurable
  pain of the Father be stilled
Through the liberation of all beings from the tragedy
  of thy withdrawal.
For thine is the homeland, and the boundless wisdom,
  and the all-merciful grace,
For all and everything in the Circle of All. Amen. [35]

Here Sophia, "Our Mother," lives in darkness, but the responsibility for her condition is not due to the machinations of some spiritual being like Lucifer or Yaldabaoth or on account of her own transgressions, but because of humankind's collective amnesia. Our forgetting, that is, is the reason for her apparent imprisonment. Remembering, then, becomes resurrection, becomes restoration, becomes liberation, becomes transfiguration.

EXILES

Sophia's exile, the punishment for her sins, I would suggest, should not be read objectively, clinically, or condescendingly as a fairy tale far removed from us in space and time. Instead, I think we should read the Gnostic tragedy of Sophia while looking into a mirror, for we are the ones in exile from God, in exile from Creation, and, as a result, in exile from ourselves. The Gnostic mythos reveals itself as a form of mirror-writing: while we try to decode it, we are looking at ourselves. That's the message.

Our triune alienation from God, Creation, and ourselves, furthermore, should not be understood as three discrete alienations but as one alienation with three manifestations. To be in exile from God, that is, is to be in exile from Creation. To be in exile from both God and Creation is to be in exile from our own being. To be in exile from God, Creation, and ourselves is to live in a false universe not dissimilar from those the Gnostics

---

35 Quoted in Christopher Bamford, Introduction to *Christ and Sophia* by Valentin Tomberg, xxvii–xviii. Modified.

explore in their rich and complex mythologies. As a result of this alienation, we find ourselves in a materialistic, technocratic, and superficial universe where we can find no home, no solace, nothing real. Out of necessity, if not desperation, many (most Christians included), try to convince themselves that where we find ourselves is not our true homeland, that we will one day in a far-off future find ourselves in a promised, though murky and amorphous, imagination of heaven, the place from which we came and whither we return. Thus the consolation for the forlorn. We, then, are the true Gnostics. We wander in a supreme disconnect from reality, a disruption implicit in every variety of neurosis. As C. G. Jung diagnosed it, neurosis is a condition found when individuals "content themselves with inadequate or wrong answers to the questions of life."[36] A civilization lacking interest in ultimate questions — the existence of God, the meaning of life, the possibility of truth — is by default a civilization characterized by neurosis, by alienation from the Real. As consolation, we content ourselves with glittering abstractions: an impoverished bargain.

Once upon a time a century ago, in the aftermath of two world wars, philosophers, theologians, and artists were troubled by the problem of evil, their anxieties persisting throughout the century. Eventually, it seems, the problem of evil dissipated into a kind of malaise, a condition best treated on an individual level with psychotropic drugs, and on a collective level with the correlative soporifics of perpetual entertainment and other forms of intoxication, including the intoxication of rage. In their time, George Orwell and Aldous Huxley examined these social realities, simply extrapolating from the cultural context of the 1920s and -30s and projecting their probabilities into the future. Their warnings no longer seem as dire as they once did, probably because the tragedies they prophesied have for the most part been realized (to general acceptance and approval)

---

36 C. G. Jung, *Memories, Dreams, and Reflections*, ed, Aniela Jaffé; trans. Richard and Clara Winston, revised (New York: Vintage Books, 1989), 140.

as societies have shown themselves willing to put up with the artificial universe known as "The Land of How Things Are" for the sake of Community-Identity-Stability — though only simulacra of community, identity, and stability. But, as Huxley and Orwell so clearly stated, it is exactly thus that evil comes to rule: quietly and unobtrusively, by increments and by gradual acquiescence. Welcome to the Reign of Yaldabaoth.

The evils of the twentieth century — gas chambers, genocide, nuclear war, to mention only three — were palpable to those in the West, and their terrifying specters persisted to the end of the millennium (having since been outsourced generally, and for the most part invisibly to Western eyes, to the Middle East and Africa). As psychoanalyst Erich Neumann wrote in the years following World War II,

> The phenomenon which brands our epoch is a collective outbreak of evil in man, on a scale never before manifested in world history. The various conscious explanations — ideological, political, sociological, etc. — which, as depth psychology knows, never grasp the real cause of the matter, cannot explain away the fact that it has been possible for evil to seize hold of hundreds of millions of human beings. The old ethic of the Judeo-Christian epoch has proved itself incapable of mastering the destructive forces in man. [37]

To be sure, the devastation of the world wars caused many millions to question the validity of religion, let alone the existence of God. But, as Peter said to the Master, "My Lord, to whom shall we go? You have the words of eternal life" (John 6:68). Many preferred nothing, which ensured their absolute exile from the Real.

The roots of this malaise can be found in the rise of modernity, not as the usual bugbears secularization or atheism — which are merely symptoms — but by the path through which,

---

37 Erich Neumann, *Depth Psychology and a New Ethic*, trans. Eugene Rolfe (New York: Harper and Row, 1973), 25–26.

18

as H. J. Massingham wrote in 1942, "Christendom began to depart from Christianity, and to what extent the embryonic causes of that division have developed into the anarchic consequences of the 20th century"[38]— consequences which metastasized in the 21st. For Massingham, the only answer to such a pathology lies in the regeneration of Christianity, almost as a new religion, and this regeneration could only be through the restoration of a proper relationship to the cosmos:

> Nor can the Christian Faith (seeing there is no alternative to it) itself be rejuvenated unless it be equally shown that its own division from nature has pauperized it as an all-sufficient gospel for modern, grown-up, Western man, wrecked in the bitter sea of his delusion of self-will. The pagan story of Iggdrasil, the Tree of Life, whose roots were in the earth and topmost branches in heaven, prefigures that gospel.[39]

How much further are we estranged from the Real some eighty years later? It does not seem that the churches have learned much over the last century.

I wonder if the discovery of the treasure troves of Gnostic scriptures found at Qumran and Nag Hammadi immediately following World War II really was a "coincidence." These scriptures and the mythos they proclaim seem to me disturbingly prescient in illuminating the evils of a civilization marked by alternate realities, whether they be through video gaming, pharmacological sedation, propaganda wars, mass surveillance, or the infinite varieties of distractions at our disposal, all implicit in our estrangement from the Real. Of course, stepping into this understanding leaves one not far from slipping into conspiracy theory. But maybe, as Guido Preparata puts it, "Conspiracy theory is too important to be left to conspiracy theorists." The rebirth of Gnosticism in the twentieth century not only

---

38 H. J. Massingham, *The Tree of Life* (London: Chapman and Hall, 1943), 17.
39 Ibid.

impacted theology and biblical studies to a profound degree, but also impacted the humanities, and nowhere as powerfully as in literature and film. It also seems to have provided the capitalist-socialist archons of the present age with a productive and infinitely extensible business plan.

The science fiction writer Philip K. Dick, for example, a beautiful, prescient, and nonetheless troubled soul, drew on Gnostic ideas in his body of work, writing which serves as an extended meditation on the (mis)perception of reality and the challenges posed by the Delphic dictum, *gnôthi seauton!* ("Know thyself!"). From early in his career, Dick was preoccupied with this problem, which is at root a theological exegesis on the problem of evil, the difficulties in knowing who we really are, and how to locate the Real. Indeed, following what many would call a genuinely bizarre religious experience initiated by seeing an ichthys symbol hanging on a girl's necklace when she delivered a pizza to his house in 1974, Dick wrote what he called *The Exegesis*, an 8000-page account of the insights/dreams/visions the symbol inspired and which drifts between the profound and the hallucinogenic. In harmony with the lesson of *The Hymn of the Pearl*, Dick's experience led him into considerations of memory and memory's relationship to identity. As he writes,

> The very idea of "wake up" implies winter time and the slumbering during winter time of all life. In some fashion, however, we once were awake and then fell asleep, which is what the Greeks meant by Lethe, by forgetfulness; forgetfulness is equated with falling asleep, and waking up with anamnesis. . . . As when I felt that an Essene or someone holy who had been slumbering in me thousands of years and who possessed Sophia Pistis had awakened; the shock was of such enormity as to be beyond words to express. [40]

---

40 Philip K. Dick, *The Exegesis of Philip K. Dick*, ed. Pamela Jackson and Jonathan Lethem; Erik Davis, annotations ed. (Boston: Houghton Mifflin Harcourt, 2011), 148.

In his novel *Valis*, heavily influenced by the experiences he records in *The Exegesis*, Dick extends this idea imaginatively: "It has to do with the loss of amnesia; when forgetfulness is lost, true memory spreads out backward and forward, into the past and into the future, and also, oddly, into alternate universes; it is orthogonal as well as linear."[41] In Christian theology, we have a name for such a disruption of time: *kairos*, the timeless time of God. Of course, some point to the fact that Dick may have been suffering from mental illness, at least some form of neurosis, even a mild psychosis. I have no doubts that this may have been true. But in that light, I feel I should share a story. Once upon a time, I was talking about Joan of Arc to a priest friend of mine, concerned as I was (and I am not alone) that Joan of Arc also may have been suffering from mental illness. "Yeah," he said, "maybe she was. But what makes you think God doesn't talk to crazy people?" Dick may have been "crazy" by some standards; that doesn't mean he was wrong. On the other hand, I, along with billions of others, believe the godhead himself appears in the form of bread and wine that I then eat to make him part of me, which millions dismiss as infantile, if not completely insane. So maybe the idea of madness is relative.

Like Philip K. Dick, filmmaker Terrence Malick also draws on Gnosticism in his work, but, with Malick, Gnostic pessimism vanishes before the radiance of sophianic splendor. In his film, *The Thin Red Line* (1998), for example, it is not the case of an alternate and more real reality "somewhere else" that Malick explores. Rather, his cinematic contemplation centers on the Real-as-it-is, and that we ignore to our peril. When Private Witt (Jim Caviezel) finds himself in detention, facing court-martial, after having gone AWOL just prior to the invasion of Guadalcanal — in his absence participating in the blissful harmony with Creation of Micronesian islanders — he is forced to confront his hardened and cynical superior, Sergeant Welsh

---

41   Philip K. Dick, *Valis* (1981; reprt. New York: Vintage Books, 1991), 121.

(Sean Penn). Welsh tells him, "In this world . . . a man himself is nothing. And there ain't no world but this one." Witt replies, "You're wrong there, Top. I seen another world. . . . Sometimes I think it was just my imagination." With the islanders, he witnessed a paradisal world of a community in harmony with God and with Nature, while the "real world" of politics and war invites nothing but confusion, violence, hatred, and an overarching insanity. Indeed, Welsh's cynicism is simply the armor he wears to protect himself from absolute despair. But let's be clear: there is another world.

In their last conversation in the film, following the harrowing ordeal of the battle over Guadalcanal and having witnessed many of their comrades and alleged enemies killed or wounded, Welsh mockingly asks Witt, "You still believing in the beautiful light, are you?" after which he mutters, "How do you do that?" Witt responds, "I still see a spark in you." The spark, as we have seen, is an important concept in Gnosticism (and also appears in Jacob Boehme's mysticism). Welsh, as armored and jaded as he is, still retains the intrinsic divinity that is the birthright of every human, despite our efforts to extinguish it. Later in the film, after Welsh buries Witt's body in the jungle, Welsh speaks to the makeshift grave, "Where's your spark now?" Is he speaking ironically? Or does he think Witt can actually hear him? Perhaps his question is simply the palimpsest of childhood faith. Perhaps. Malick's *oeuvre* returns again and again to the contrast between modern, materialist insanity and the paradisal realm that shimmers alongside it. These themes are particularly prevalent in *The Tree of Life* (2011) and *Knight of Cups* (2015), the latter of which uses *The Hymn of the Pearl* as its narrative scaffolding, even quoting from it at length.

Dick and Malick offer us two ways to think about the Gnostic universe we inhabit. Is it merely a matter of *knowing*, as it is in Dick, that somehow realizing the world as it has been constructed around us is false can be enough? Or is it, as we find in Malick, not a question of knowing, but of participating in the cosmos *as the Real* that we simultaneously understand there is another world: this one? Both illustrate variations on exile, but Malick shows us the liberation of Sophia from exile is at its core a liberation of human beings from their exile from the Real. Sophia, that is, is not the one in exile. We are. Our exile is made all the more devastating by the fact that we think we are free. "Freedom," to be sure, is the byword of our age, and the desire for "liberation" from the constraints of God and of Nature is made painfully real in our desire to be liberated from God and Nature in our bodies. Elsewhere, I have called this "the technological colonization of the human person," and there certainly is much to be considered concerning this in the diabolical dream that is transhumanism. But to think a "transhuman" epoch would be distinguished by human-computer hybrids as our new overlords seems a rather clunky and adolescent way to imagine its realization. More significant, I think, is the growing trend, sold to us by propaganda, of liberating ourselves from gender and sex by the employment of surgeries and hormone regimens: a far more effective way to see how easily we can be exiled from Nature and, therefore, from God. This is but one example of how the Archons of This Age entrap us in a net of unreality. But we go into bondage willingly: voluntary exile, after all, is the most effective. And this, I believe, is the most tragic piece of evidence pointing to the false Gnostic universe which we now inhabit. We are all of us Yaldabaoths in the making. *And it's all about the making.* Yaldabaoth deluded himself into thinking he was the Creator God. Are we so different?

The Hymn of the Pearl, however, does have a happy ending. After the Prince forgets his origin and his mission, his father, worrying that his son is tarrying too long in the Land of Egypt, sends him a letter. The letter transforms into an eagle, and when it arrives the young man kisses it. At that point, the eagle "turned into speech altogether."[42]

---

42   *The Hymn of the Robe of Glory*, line 52.

From Us — King of Kings, thy Father,
And thy Mother, Queen of the Dawn-land,
And from Our Second, thy Brother —
To thee, Son, down in Egypt, Our Greeting!
Up and arise from thy sleep,
Give ear to the words of Our Letter!
Remember that thou art a King's son;
See whom thou hast served in thy slavedom.
Bethink thyself of the Pearl
For which thou didst journey to Egypt.
Remember thy Glorious Robe,
Thy Splendid Mantle remember,
To put on and wear as adornment,
When thy Name may be read in the Book of the Heroes,
And with Our Successor, thy Brother,
Thou may be Heir in Our Kingdom. [43]

The Prince remembers who he is and why he was sent into the Land of Egypt.

Remembering. It all begins with remembering.

---

43 Ibid., lines 41–48.

2

Of What Body.
Through What Years.
In What Light.

THE SOPHIOLOGICAL
STRUCTURE OF MARRIAGE

When Love walks in the room,
Everybody stand up.
~:The Pretenders, "Message of Love"

IN SUMMER OF 1658, THE ALCHEMIST AND
Anglican priest Thomas Vaughan dreamt of his late wife,
Rebecca, who had died at the age of about twenty-five
that year on the seventeenth of April. He recorded the dream
in a notebook entitled *Aqua Vitæ: Non Vitis*, which also housed
notes of the many alchemical experiments he and Rebecca had
undertaken together while she lived:

> god Almightie was pleased to reveale unto mee, after a
> wonderful maner, the most blessed Estate of my deare
> Wife, partly by her self, and partly by his owne Holy spirit,
> in an Expresse discourse, which opened unto mee the
> meaning of those mysterious words of St. Paul: For wee
> know, That if our Earthly house of this Tabernacle &c. [1]

---

1 *Thomas and Rebecca Vaughan's Aqua Vitæ: Non Vitis* (British Library MS,
Sloane 1741), ed. and trans. Donald R. Dickson (Tempe, AZ: Arizona Center
of Medieval and Renaissance Studies, 2001), 202. The biblical reference
is to 2 Corinthians 5:1: "For we know that if our earthly house of this
tabernacle were dissolved, we have a building of God, an house not made
with hands, eternal in the heavens."

At the bottom of the entry, Vaughan inscribed words evocative of those from the marriage service: "*Quos Deus Conjunxit, Quis seperabit?*" Who will separate those whom God has joined together? Vaughan placed much confidence in the dreams he had of his deceased wife, touched as they sometimes were with the spirit of prophecy:

> The Dreame I writt on the fore-going page is not to bee neglected: for my deare wife a few nights before, appeared to mee in my Sleepe, and fore-told mee the Death of my deare Father, and since it is really come to passe, for hee is dead, and gone to my mercifull and most loving God, who useth not to deale such mercies to all men: and who was pleased to impart it to mee by my deare Wife, to assure mee shee was a Saint in his Holy Heavens, being thus imployed for an Angell, and a messenger of the god of my Salvation: To him bee all prayse and glorie ascribed in Jesus for ever. [2]

It is telling that even after Rebecca's death, Vaughan continued to sign entries in the notebook "T. R. V." for "Thomas and Rebecca Vaughan."

The cause of Rebecca's death is unknown — her husband only notes that she sickened on the 16th of April and died the following evening[3] — but speculation has not been silent. Vaughan himself died on the 27th of February 1665 (1666 by modern reckoning) following an alchemical mishap involving mercury, so it is not out of the question that Rebecca's death was likewise linked to experiments in "chymistry." But that's hardly the only possibility.

One person engaged in such speculation was the poet and essayist Kenneth Rexroth. Rexroth, ever a bold and imaginative thinker, read the Vaughans' experimental life as inextricably linked with both their spiritual and sexual lives. For him, alchemy operates via a kind of sympathetic magic, a doctrine

---

2   Ibid.
3   Ibid., 243.

of signatures, which, when perfected, enacts a simultaneously spiritual and physical *hieros gamos*, sacred marriage, which "literally fecundates the earth [and] at the same time achieves salvation for the soul."[4] He reads Rebecca as Thomas's *Soror Mystica* and suggests that Rebecca's death may have been the result of what Eastern esoteric philosophy calls "the raising of the kundalini," as the tantric literature is replete with warnings about awakening this force by the uninitiated. "Thomas and Rebecca Vaughan," writes Rexroth, "wrapped in entranced embrace at the Pinner of Wakefield, were, it is true, blundering into a region of revelation which they little understood and which, it would seem, eventually destroyed them both."[5]

I am not willing to affirm Rexroth's diagnosis, interesting as it is, but I do think he points to something vital, though sadly lacking, from Christian consideration: the possibility of a sacred marriage and a concomitant possibility of a sacred sexuality within that marriage. To be perfectly honest, Christianity has a conflicted history with both.

The reasons for Christianity's complicated history concerning marriage and sexuality are many and diffuse. Preeminent among them is St. Paul's admonition in 1 Corinthians 7 that it is better to remain celibate than to marry, though better to marry than to "burn."[6] This may seem very straightforward a pronouncement, but take into consideration Paul's context for writing and the clarity of the statement takes on a different connotation. First of all, Paul was writing in anticipation of the *Parousia*, believing the Second Coming of Christ was imminent. Within such a time frame, of course marrying would be superfluous.[7]

---

4   Kenneth Rexroth, *With Eye and Ear* (New York: Herder and Herder, 1970), 8.
5   Ibid., 9.
6   πυροῦσθαι (*pyrousthai*)
7   See, for example, Gail Corrington Streete, "Discipline and Disclosures: Paul's Apocalyptic Asceticism in 1 Corinthians," in *Vision and Persuasion: Rhetorical Dimension of Apocalyptic Discourse*, ed. Greg Carey and L. Gregory Bloomquist (St. Louis, MO: Chalice Press, 1999), 81–94.

But that's not what happened: not yet, and not in Paul's time. Nevertheless, in the beaten ways of theology, such a conceptual release took on a life of its own, much like an ideological invasive species.

The late-classical era, of course, had ample models of the ascetic eschewal of sexual intercourse and marriage, and many so-called pagan religions and philosophies also participated in the profound error that the spiritual is superior to the physical. Therefore, according to this view, the renunciation of marriage and sexual intercourse was unarguably a higher calling. The idea haunts Neoplatonism and various strains of Gnosticism and was a feature of the priesthoods of the Mysteries of Isis and the Great Mother. Though outside of Paul's very specialized case in 1 Corinthians, there is nothing in the Gospels or Acts that suggests that an ascetical and celibate priesthood was a more exalted form of the Christian life. Nevertheless, as Christianity grew and some of its adherents sought legitimacy in the eyes of the greater culture, an unacknowledged mimesis stole into the Christian psyche.

The patristic literature is fairly tumid with examples of this anxiety, which was all too often projected onto women. Tertullian, the patristic version of a hotheaded loudmouth, harangues the fairer sex in his diatribe, De cultu feminarum (On the Adornment of Women): "Do you not know you are an Eve? The sentence of God on this sex of yours lives in this age; the guilt must of necessity live, too. You are the devil's gateway: you are the unsealer of that forbidden tree: you are the first deserter of the divine law."[8] He even blames women for the crucifixion of Christ! And he wasn't talking about the temptations found in good cooking. Furthermore, the story (perhaps apocryphal) of Origen castrating himself in order to draw closer to God does very little to ameliorate the notion that the Christian psychology of sex has been askew since the

---

8 De cultu feminarum, I.I.

earliest times.[9] And I'm afraid I have never quite forgiven St. Augustine for sending away his common-law wife and mother of his son during the course of his conversion and his attendant race to become holy.[10] It may be that the Bishop of Hippo never completely transcended the dualistic Manichaeism of his youth. Indeed, much of the history of Christianity has been and continues to be haunted by such a dualism, often couched in "the earth is not our real home" falsities uttered by professing Christians *ad nauseum*.

Such binary cultural assumptions likewise carried into the social order and the establishment of social hierarchies. Of particular importance here is the polarity between clergy and laity. Whatever the original intent (and even a cursory reading of Acts of the Apostles suggests it was not), the distinction between clergy and laity, and especially once Christianity gained legitimacy in the eyes of the Roman Empire, more and more became one of initiates and *profani*. To be sure, the characteristics of the Christian initiatic orders in relation to the laity were of not the same timbre as those between initiates in the pagan Mysteries and the uninitiated. Nevertheless, just as the Church, once it was named the state religion, engaged in a mimesis of the Mysteries and court ceremonial by adopting some of their ritual currency, so did it develop a social stratification very foreign to the generally egalitarian nature of the early Church, in which there "is neither Jew nor Gentile, neither slave nor free, nor is there male and female, for you are all one in Christ Jesus" (Galatians 3:28). Social orders seem to like having an elite class, and for millennia the ecclesial hierarchy has served such a function in the Church. This celibate elite class, then, more or less interpreted the world — and especially the Church — though a celibate lens. Nowhere has this been more evident than in the tradition of commentary on the Song of Songs.

---

9   Reported by Eusebius, *Historia Ecclesiae*, 6.8.
10 *Confessions* 6.15. He never mentions her name.

THE SONG OF SONGS

The Song of Songs, such an anomaly in the canon of scripture with its deep and affirmative eros, offers us a glimpse into a sacred sexuality of the marriage chamber that, through most of its history, official Christendom has ignored, forcing allegorical readings upon the plain meaning of a text that even Benedict XVI at last conceded was "intended for a Jewish wedding feast and meant to exult conjugal love."[11] Nevertheless, the primary interpretive mode when confronting such an erotically charged text has been to read it as an allegory for God's relationship with the soul (or the Church). The Song of Songs, that is, was co-opted by a monasticism which wrested a healthy Christian relationship to sexuality away from the laity, veritably turning the Song into a Lacanian *objet petit a*, an unattainable object of desire. As Peter Dronke explains, "Theologians, predictably, either ignored the erotic wellspring of such language or recognized it only in order to reject it. Yet inevitably this *fons hortorum* continued to flow in a poetic *hortus conclusus*, where mystical and sensual expression and imagery grew together, a garden that was to be of lasting importance for the European imagination."[12]

In fact, the Song was the most-often commented upon text in the medieval cloister, a trajectory that was set in late-antiquity with Origen (how often that name comes up!). Origen offers a confusedly transgendered reading of the Song as an "epithalamium . . . which Solomon wrote in the form of a drama and sang *under the figure of the Bride*, about to wed and burning with heavenly love towards her Bridegroom, who is the Word of God."[13] No one unfamiliar with the traditional allegorical interpretation of the Song would ever come to such a conclusion.

11 *Deus Caritas Est* (God Is Love) (2006), 8.
12 Peter Dronke, "*The Song of Songs* and Medieval Love Lyric," in *The Bible and Medieval Culture*, ed. W. Lourdaux and D. Verhelst (Leuven University Press, 1979), 236–62, at 242.
13 Origen, *The Song of Songs Commentary and Homilies*, trans. R. P. Lawson (Westminster: Newman Press, 1957), 21. My emphasis.

Talk about a *violence du texte*. It's not that Origen doesn't know about the plain sense of the poem. He most certainly does:

> But if any man who lives only after the flesh should approach it [i.e., the Song], to such a one the reading of this scripture will be the occasion of no small hazard and danger. For he, not knowing how to hear love's language in purity and with chaste ears, will twist the whole manner of his hearing of it away from the inner spiritual man and on to the outward and carnal; and he will be turned away from the spirit to the flesh, and he will fasten carnal desires in himself, and it will seem to be the Divine Scriptures that are thus urging him on to fleshly lust. [14]

I assume Origen is referring to the same Divine Scriptures that tell the survivors of the Flood to be fruitful and multiply. But I digress.

The anxiety inhering Origen's encounter with the Song was not particular to him, as it characterizes theological commentary from late antiquity through modernity. Some, such as Theodore of Mopsuestia (c. 350 – 428) and Jovinian (c. 400), not to mention Marcion, held the poem to be a great celebration of human love, but they were generally maligned and in the minority. Martin Luther, on the other hand, who generally railed against allegory as hermeneutical method, calling it "a beautiful harlot, who proves herself especially seductive with idle men," [15] nevertheless turned to allegory when faced with the Song. Apparently, when it came to the Song, allegory was one beautiful harlot Luther couldn't resist.

One cannot fail to observe, however, that all the figures mentioned so far were professional theologians and clerics writing for other theologians and clerics — and, with the exception of Luther, in manuscript. Very few people were literate

14   Ibid., 22.
15   Quoted in George L. Scheper, "Reformation Attitudes toward Allegory and the Song of Songs," PMLA 89, no 3 (May 1974): 551.

in those centuries and wouldn't have been able to read the Song itself, let alone commentaries on it, were such available. So it is important to take into consideration the rise of print culture in, especially, the fifteenth and sixteenth centuries and the simultaneous increase in literacy as books become more widely available. In England alone, between 1549 and 1700 no less than one-hundred-thirty editions of the Song — in commentary, paraphrases, or poetic renderings — found their way into print, many in octavo format, making them accessible to readers of relatively modest means. All of them upheld the allegorical interpretation first put forward by Origen, but this by no means suggests that this was how they were read. As Noam Flinker argues, "Although the official word of the Church loudly stipulated that the biblical text be read only as an allegory, enough evidence has survived to indicate that other readings continued to remain available."[16]

The Song of Songs is certainly one of the most beautiful evocations of eros ever recorded, and I consider it an act of Divine Providence that it is enshrined in scripture not only as allegory (which is a valid *secondary* reading) but as approval and celebration of the erotic energies that radiate from sexuality between man and woman within the temple of marriage:

> Let my beloved come into his garden, and eat the fruit
> of his apple trees. I am come into my garden, O my sister,
> my spouse, I have gathered my myrrh, with my aromat-
> ical spices: I have eaten the honeycomb with my honey,
> I have drunk my wine with my milk: eat, O friends,
> and drink, and be inebriated, my dearly beloved. (5:1)

The Song shimmers with sensual delights that transport the reader in imaginative arousal. This cannot be denied — yet it has been. In fact, the denial of precisely this fact has crippled religious consciousness and, by extension, produced a psychological

---

16 Noam Flinker, *The Song of Songs in English Renaissance Literature: The Kisses of Their Mouths* (Cambridge, UK: D. S. Brewer, 2000), 19.

virus that disfigures when it doesn't kill. Truly, if Freud hadn't existed, it would have been necessary to invent him.

What we have in the Song is an imaginative *hieros gamos*, a picture of the sacred marriage, a holiness that overshadows every marriage between man and woman in the Judeo-Christian traditions. In fact, some have even contemplated whether the Song might be a liturgical text of sacred marriage, the ritual context of which is now lost to posterity.[17] But, regardless of whether or not the Song was the script of the *hieros gamos*, we should treat it as our own guide now. My claim is that the Song of Songs is a kind of Judeo-Christian *Kama Sutra*: not that it offers a variety of techniques for achieving sexual union and pleasure, but that it presents us with the archetype of the sacred marriage in all of its delights and its delicacies, its anxieties and its intimacies.

Even ignoring its erotic content, the Song is unique among biblical texts for a number of reasons. For one, the Song issues no commandments or commentary on law. For another, man and woman stand on an equal footing in the poem: the Shulamite is not subordinate to her beloved, the systole and diastole of presence and absence rendering them equals. In addition, the lovers don't even appear to subjugate nature, but are "virtually interchangeable with it."[18] Neither is the Song subversive, as Alicia Ostriker observes: "It is not a protest poem, it is not anti-patriarchal; rather, it lives in an alternative dimension, as if patriarchy did not exist."[19] The poem, furthermore, can be said to return the lovers (and the reader) to prelapsarian Eden when the conjugal act had not yet been compromised by concupiscence, a literary act of regeneration

---

17 See, for example, G. Lloyd Carr, "Is *The Song of Songs* a 'Sacred Marriage' Drama?," *Journal of the Evangelical Theological Society* 22, no. 2 (1979): 103–14.
18 Alicia Ostriker, "A Holy of Holies: *The Song of Songs* as Countertext," in *The Song of Songs: A Feminist Companion to the Bible* (Second Series), ed. Athalya Brenner and Carole R. Fontaine (Sheffield, UK: Sheffield Academic Press, 2000), 36–54, at 43.
19 Ibid., 48.

and restoration. Perhaps most startlingly, apart from a nearly invisible secondary allusion at 8:6 that most translations gloss over, the Song never mentions God. Yet divinity shines through every syllable of the text, in Rexroth's words, "Of what body. Through what years. In what light."[20]

THE THINGS OF GOD

Some have argued that some religious proscriptions on sexuality in both Judaism and Christianity are not based on a fear of sexuality as a species of spiritual pollution, as one might find in some forms of Gnosticism, but due to the fact that the creative power of God is present in the procreative powers manifest in conjugal union. Because procreation is a property of God, one must be purified after having touched these mysteries — whether they be of sexual congress or of menses. This is, I admit, a useful way to think about it. Unfortunately, that is not how it works out in reality, and often religious rubrics reach absurd conclusions. As noted earlier, Evdokimov observes that "Certain forms of asceticism that prescribe avoiding one's own mother, and even animals of the female sex, say a great deal about the loss of psychic balance."[21] Indeed, the practice of not allowing women — and even animals of the female sex — on Mount Athos (clearly alluded to by Evdokimov) is pathology writ large. A friend of mine, to share a tale, once visited Athos. He was happily married and with young children. Nevertheless, monks on Athos tried to get him to abandon his marriage and its sacramental bond and join their fraternity. They assured him they could "work things out" for him. Absolute insanity. Again, from Evdokimov: "It is with the hermits that the 'woman question' becomes most current, reducing it to its 'passionate' aspect and compromising it forever. Certain theologians deem

---

20 Kenneth Rexroth, "The Phoenix and the Tortoise," in *The Phoenix and the Tortoise* (Norfolk, CT: New Directions, 1944), 16.
21 Paul Evdokimov, *Woman and the Salvation of the World: A Christian Anthropology on the Charisms of Women*, trans. Anthony P. Gythiel (Crestwood, NY: St. Vladimir's Seminary Press, 1994), 26.

it useless to propagate the human race; they reduce marriage to the one aim of avoiding incontinence. This is why a conjugal love that is too passionate borders on adultery."[22] Is it any wonder that there is confusion about sexuality — even within the precincts of marriage — in the Christian psyche? This insanity lies deep in the Christian consciousness, as this statement from a fourteenth-century Encyclopedia of Canon Law makes only too clear in its instructions for married archpriests:

> The divine Fathers of the Sixth Council in their twelfth canon forbid archpriests after ordination to live at all with their legal wives who were joined to them by marriage before ordination; and state "we do not decree this for the abolition of what was legislated by the sacred apostles in their fifth canon, but to bring about the Church's advancement toward that which is better...."
> They say it is necessary for archpriests who govern their lives with strict chastity, not only to abstain from sexual intercourse with other women, but also with their own wives.... Next, they apply the penalty of defrocking to those who do not observe the canon.[23]

Today, for some reason, married deacons and priests in even the Catholic Church are advised to avoid sexual intercourse the night before participating in the Mass or Divine Liturgy. Jewish tradition, on the other hand, argues that husband and wife uniting in loving embrace on the Sabbath are participating in God's union with his Shekinah and are thereby simultaneously assisting in the salvation of the world. Which approach sounds the more sane? It should be clear that a serious disruption occurred during the growth of Christianity. The Protestant

---

22 Paul Evdokimov, *The Sacrament of Love: The Nuptial Mystery in the Light of the Orthodox Tradition*, trans. Olivier Clement (Crestwood, NY: St. Vladimir's Seminary Press, 1995), 17.

23 Patrick Demitrios Viscuso, *Sexuality, Marriage, and Celibacy in Byzantine Law: Selections form a Fourteenth-Century Encyclopedia of Canon Law and Theology, The Alphabetical Collection of Matthew Blastares* (Brookline, MA: Holy Cross Orthodox Press, 2008), 131.

Reform tried to address this, of course, but the disorder is in the grain.

The Christian exaltation of virginity, particularly in the presumed perpetual virginity of the Theotokos, no doubt reifies the problematic of married sexuality here under discussion, and has resulted in what Evdokimov (and anyone else with a gift for clear thinking) can see as a depreciation of marriage.[24] The archetype of the celibate Holy Family is one no Christian family could hope to live up to. To be sure, to interpret the Holy Family as celibates might be a way to foreground their absolute otherness, but the image is an empty signifier, at least as far as actual Christian families are concerned. And while it would be apparent to any high school theology student that the marriage of Mary and Joseph, if not consummated, would not be a valid marriage under a Catholic rubric, theologians have found ways to wiggle out of this one as well, despite the problematic utterances in the gospels of Matthew (13:55) and Mark (6:3) about Jesus's brothers and sisters. But when celibates and monastics write the rules, they often write in their own image and likeness, unconscious though the process may be. With the rise of monasticism (how that was derived from the communities described in Acts I'll never know), the celibate life became held out as the "highest" or "ideal" form of (not) living in this world — maybe not in theory, but certainly in practice. This is clericalism writ large. And all the sins of clericalism, I contend, flow from this one.

While it is true that clerics and theologians throughout the first centuries of Christianity were not against the idea of marriage (though about sexuality within marriage, things were a little more complicated), the unspoken primacy of virginity and celibacy in the Christian cultural imaginary reigned unchecked for the most part until Luther. Nevertheless, various attempts at rehabilitation appeared over the course of the

---

24 Paul Evdokimov, *The Sacrament of Love*, 16.

history of Christianity. It could be argued that Protestantism prevailed in this rehabilitation, but, in fact, the demotion of matrimony from its proper rank as a Sacrament only succeeded in further secularizing the West. The metastasis of an absolute secularization eventually led to the reality of marriage being almost entirely flattened in the early twenty-first century as it lost even the assumption that it is only something that can be realized in the union of a man and a woman.

ATTEMPTS AT REHABILITATION

Something marvelous happened in Western Europe during the late medieval period: joy entered the world. Splendor began to shine through the universe, quite literally via the introduction of Gothic architecture with its aesthetics and theology of light inspired by Pseudo-Dionysius, and figuratively through the rise of Marian devotion and the growing popularity of the Rosary. In addition, joy spread as well through the languages of love uttered by the troubadours and *Brautmystik*, which reached their apotheosis in St. Francis of Assisi and Dante. This was the Beautiful Revolution and, especially in the case of the troubadours, influenced Christian ideas of love and marriage.

The Troubadours

Troubadour poetry, with its emphasis on the beloved Lady and permeated by an atmosphere of a nearly Platonic divide between the physical and the spiritual, certainly seems to have been influenced by the Sufi poetics of Qawwali, which often collapse the languages of love for God and a more earthly beloved. In Sufi poetics and mysticism, writes Robert Briefault, "Divine love cannot be understood by him who has not experienced the transports of profane love."[25] The eleventh-century Sufi poet Ibn Hazam illustrates this notion beautifully:

---

25 Robert S. Briefault, *The Troubadours*, trans. by the author, ed. Lawrence F. Koons (Bloomington, IN: Indiana University Press, 1965), 26.

I see a human form, but when I think more deeply
(It seems) a body from higher spheres!
Blessed be He who balanced the origin of His creation
So that you are the beautiful natural light!
I have no doubt that you are a spirit drawn to us
By a conjoining resemblance of the souls.[26]

Clearly, Plato's *Symposium* informs Ibn Hazam to a profound
degree, and indirectly influenced the Troubadours through
Sufism (Plato's works had yet to arrive in the West). In addition,
it has been argued by Gaston Paris among others that European folk religion (both Christian and pagan) influenced the
love languages of the troubadours.[27] As Ezra Pound phrases
it, "Provençal song is never wholly disjunct from pagan rites
of May Day."[28]

Much has been made of the troubadours' influence on
modern notions of love and marriage, most notably Denis de
Rougemont's mid-twentieth-century exercise in psychological
projection known as *Love in the Western World*. Sad was the day,
laments de Rougemont, when arranged marriages fell into
disfavor and marriages based on love came to prominence.
Particularly annoyed at the love complications of *Tristan and
Iseult*, de Rougemont complains, "The Romance misses no
opportunity of disparaging the social institution of marriage
and of disparaging husbands."[29] Well, I don't know about
that. It seems to me that de Rougemont — and, indeed, most
scholars on the troubadours — misses an important point: not
all marriages in medieval Europe were arranged under such
decidedly political terms as the fictional marriage of Iseult and

---

26 Ibn Hazam, A Book Containing the Risāla Known as The Dove's Neck-
Ring about Love and Lovers, trans. and ed. A. R. Nykl (1931; reprt. Mansfield
Center, CT: Martino Publishing, 2014), 13.
27 Gaston Paris, "Etudes sur les romans de la table ronde: Lancelot du
Lac," Romania 12 (1883): 459 – 534, at 499 – 502.
28 Ezra Pound, The Spirit of Romance, 2nd ed. (Norfolk, CT: New Directions, 1952), 90.
29 Denis de Rougemont, Love in the Western World, trans. Montgomery
Belgion, revised (Greenwich, CT: Fawcett, 1958), 35.

King Mark and the actual marriages of the medieval nobility. The peasantry, for example, had far more latitude in marrying for love than did the nobility, and we cannot rule out at least a modicum of mimetic desire in what troubadour poetry and chivalric Romance disclose about love. And this should come as no surprise. Briefault argues that troubadour poetry, despite its aristocratic veneer and appropriation by the nobility, "was, from first to last, in its origin, development and poetry, essentially an art of jongleurs of humble extraction."[30] The troubadours, then, were influenced by their jealousy of peasant marriage.

The troubadours' intuitions are, in fact, more Christian than the idea of arranged marriages, for they are supra-political, antinomic, transcending as they do the claims of the world upon lovers and ascending to a Christian metaphysics of love that is equal parts *eros* and *caritas*. This is clear in how easily the rhetoric of the troubadour for his lady could be transposed to a religious poetics simply by changing her name to that of the Virgin Mary.[31] The troubadour Bernardt de Ventadorn's verses are a fine example of how the distinctions between sacred and profane love dissolve in poetic *sfumato*:

> Good lady, I ask you nothing at all
> Except to make me your servant,
> For I'll serve you as I would a good Lord,
> And never ask for another reward.
> So here I am at your command,
> A frank, humble heart, courtly and glad!
> You're surely not a lion or bear
> Who'd slay me when I surrender![32]

The language of the *Brautmystik* of the later medieval period, especially that of the Beguines, likewise straddles the physical and spiritual worlds, illuminating the eros that undergirds the

---

30 Robert S. Briefault, *The Troubadours*, 89.
31 Ibid., 154–55.
32 *Troubadour Poems from the South of France*, trans. William D. Paden and Frances Freeman Paden (Cambridge, UK: D. S. Brewer, 2007), 81.

cosmos. As Denys Turner observes, eros "is the dynamic of the soul's return to God, is one and the same with the erotic overflow from God which is our creation."[33] A song from Mechthild of Magdeburg's *The Flowing Light of the Godhead*, in which God is the speaker, illustrates this divine eros beautifully:

> When I shine, you shall glow,
> When I flow, you shall become wet,
> When you sigh, you draw my divine heart to you.
> When you weep in longing for me, I take you in my arms.
> But when you love, we two become one being.
> And when we two are one being,
> Then we can never be parted.
> Rather, a blissful abiding
> Prevails between us.[34]

Once the divine ravishment takes place, according to Marguerite Porete, the soul is annihilated in love, and the demarcations between human and divine love break down:

> This Soul, says Love, has six wings like the Seraphim. She no longer wants anything that comes by a mediary. This is the proper being of the Seraphim; there is no mediary between their love and the divine Love. They always possess newness without a mediary, and so also for this Soul: for she does not seek divine knowledge among the masters of this age, but in truly despising the world and herself. Great God, how great a difference there is between a gift from a lover to a beloved through a mediary and a gift that is between lovers without a mediary.[35]

For God to be touched by eros, what Plato in the *Symposium* describes as a lack, implies that God also suffers a lack. Indeed,

---

33 Denys Turner, *Eros and Allegory: Medieval Exegesis of the Song of Songs* (Cistercian Publications, 1995), 49.
34 Mechthild of Magdeburg, *The Flowing Light of the Godhead*, trans. Frank Tobin (New York, NY: Paulist Press, 1998), 76.
35 Marguerite Porete, *The Mirror of Simple Souls*, trans. Ellen L. Babinksy (New York, NY: Paulist Press, 1993), 83.

the beginning chapters of Genesis can be read as a meditation on the eros of God's lack, a metaphysical desire that ever
reaches towards fulfillment: first with the stages of Creation;
then with the creation of Eve, prefaced by the statement "It is
not good that the man should be alone." In the first Creation
story, God says, "Let us make man in our image, after our
likeness . . . male and female created he them" (1:26 – 27). To
whom does he speak? Is it not Sophia? And is his relationship
to Sophia not evidence of eros? God's divine eros inheres the
Creation from its inception and the participation of male with
female is intrinsic to this eros. Indeed, C. G. Jung even went
so far as to describe the Assumption and Coronation of Mary
as a divine nuptial celebration:

> A consummation of the *mysterium coniunctionis* can be
> expected only when the unity of spirit, soul, and body
> is made one with the original *unus mundus*. This third
> stage of the *coniunctio* was depicted [in alchemy] after
> the manner of the Assumption and Coronation of Mary,
> in which the Mother of God represents the body. The
> Assumption is really a wedding feast, the Christian ver-
> sion of the *hierosgamos*. [36]

The yearning of God for completion is the eros which defines
being. Eros imbues mysticism — in the *Symposium*, in *Brautmystik*, in spiritual alchemy, in Sufism — as it imbues the Song
of Songs, and as it imbues LIFE, because eros is an ontological
reality, an integral structure of the cosmos.

Ralph Cudworth

The place of marriage in the Christian landscape, especially
its position among the Sacraments or Mysteries in the traditional churches, as I noted, was further compromised or

---

36   C. G. Jung, *Mysterium Coniuntionis: An Inquiry into the Separation and
Synthesis of Psychic Opposites in Alchemy*, 2nd ed., trans. R. F. C. Hull, Volume
14 of *Collected Works of* C. G. Jung (Princeton, NJ: Princeton University Press,
1963), 465 – 66.

complicated with the coming of the Protestant Reformation, which uniformly demoted matrimony from its dignity as a Sacrament. Nevertheless, a rehabilitation of this view in Protestant contexts was not altogether absent.

The Cambridge Platonist Ralph Cudworth did precisely this in his pamphlet The Union of Christ and His Church in Shadow (1642). Cudworth bewails the fact that Protestants, in seeking to reform the Catholic understanding of the Sacraments by reduction to only two, may have overcompensated when it comes to marriage and ignored "that Mystical Notion that is contained in it."[37] Cudworth, drawing on long-held theological tradition, reads the marriage of Christ and the Church as archetype and marriage between man and wife as type. For Cudworth, "The Union between Christ and the Church, thus Adumbrated and Shadowed out in the Union of Man and Wife is a great Mystery."[38] In addition to Christian tradition, he draws on ideas from Zoroastrianism and pagan antiquity to illustrate his point, but nowhere so powerfully as in his meditation on kabbalistic understandings of the spiritual meaning of marriage. His discussion of the bath kol or "Daughter of the Voice" in the Kabbalah is particularly telling in the manner in which it evokes a sophiological intuition regarding his subject:

> There is a Propriety or Sephirah in God, which is called Col or Universitas, because it is the Foundation of the Universe; and another Sephirah which is called Bath, or Filia, that floweth from him, and by this doth he guide and govern the World: and this is that which is called in the Song of Songs, Callah, that is, Sponsa, and it is that which our Wisemen have called in many places Cheneseth Israel. Here we see, Tipheret is also called Col, or Universitas, which name may very well agree to

37 R. C. [Ralph Cudworth], The Union of Christ and His Church in Shadow (London, 1642).
38 Ibid., 6.

Christ also, in whom were conceived the Idea's of the whole World, and by whom the Worlds were made; and Malcuth, or Cheneseth Israel, is called not only Callah *Sponsa*, but also Both *Filia*,, which may very well agree to the Church likewise, which is not only Spouse of Christ, but also his Daughter, flowing out from him, as *Eve* that was made out of *Adams* side, and afterward united to him, was his Wife, his Sister, and his Daughter. [39]

From these insights, and turning again to Plato in the *Symposium*, Cudworth proposes that marriage is a type of union that effects the regeneration of the archetypal bisexual union of Adam-Eve prior to Eve's separation. This notion is an important one in Jacob Boehme, and Cudworth was no doubt familiar with the German mystic's ideas. The restoration of the androgynous original (so important in Jung's notion of *anima* and *animus*) is central to the mystery of marriage for Cudworth. After quoting the *Symposium* on Zeus's separation of the androgynous original type of humanity, Cudworth connects it to Christianity:

They are incomparable words, expressing in the Type exactly according to the Scripture-Notion of the Nature of Marriage, but yet so, as looking also beyond that, they aime at some further Mystery. viz, *Hinc nimirum ex illo tempore mutuus hominibus innatus est amor* PRISCÆ NATURÆ CONCILIATOR, *annitens* VNUM EX DUOBUS *efficere*, (what could be more like that of the Scripture, *They two shall be one Flesh*). [40]

He further uses the Kabbalah to reinforce this idea:

But if we would have a true and genuine Interpretation of this Jewish Tradition, we must have recourse to the Jewish Authors themselves, and especially to the Masters of the Cabala; and they will tell us, that here

---

39 Ibid., 12.
40 Ibid., 22. "Thus, from that time, the changed men had an innate love [*eros*] for the first nature, striving to make one of two," from *Symposium* 191. Also quoting Ephesians 5:31.

also by Adam and Eve are mystically signified Tipheret and Malcuth . . . that were at first both one Sephirah, as it were Male and Female together, but afterward were parted asunder into two from being so conjoyned; but then were united together againe as Man and Wife.[41]

What Cudworth says here — not to mention Plato and the Kabbalah — is in absolute congruence with Catholic tradition (if not practice), as Benedict XVI has written,

From the standpoint of creation, eros directs man toward marriage, to a bond which is unique and definitive; thus, and only thus, does it fulfill its deepest purpose. . . . Marriage based on exclusive and definitive love becomes the icon of the relationship between God and his people and vice versa. God's way of loving becomes the measure of human love. This close connection between eros and marriage in the Bible has practically no equivalent in extra-biblical literature.[42]

Emanuel Swedenborg

Another Protestant who tried to reimagine the post-Reform picture of marriage was the polymath and mystic Emanuel Swedenborg (1688 – 1772). A successful inventor and scientist, Swedenborg began receiving aleatory spiritual experiences at the age of fifty-three in which he saw the dead, conversed with angels and demons, and received visions of and messages from the spiritual worlds. Among the many revelations he received, a number of them concerned the nature of marriage, which he believed, contrary to most theological opinion in his day or our own, extended — or could extend — beyond the grave.

41   Ibid., 24. Moshe Idel, as we have seen, discusses the same motif in Kabbalah in what he calls "the Pseudo-Aristotelian dictum" ("the first in thought is the last in action"). "This is exemplified, among other things, by the creation of the first couple initially as a unified entity; its subsequent separation; and then the reunion of the couple, which was conceived to be the initial divine intention." See his *The Privileged Divine Feminine in Kabbalah* (Berlin: De Gruyter, 2019), 67.
42   *Encyclical Letter of the Supreme Pontiff Benedict XVI: Deus Caritas Est*, 11.

Though the circumstances of Swedenborg's insights into marriage are nothing but extraordinary, their message is not all that idiosyncratic in the panorama of Christian theology. First of all, he holds to the doctrine that human marriage is a shadow of the marriage of Christ and the Church, though he goes further than most theologians in asserting a permanence to Christian marriage that others were reluctant to pursue. Fully cognizant of Jesus's admonition that in heaven "they are not given in marriage" (Matt 22:30), Swedenborg nevertheless affirms the metaphysical reality obtained in true marriage:

> By spiritual nuptials conjunction with the Lord is meant, and this is effected on earth; and when it has been effected on earth it has been effected in the heavens also; and therefore they are not married and given in marriage again in heaven.... That to be married is to be conjoined with the Lord, and that to enter into marriage is to be received into heaven by the Lord. [43]

Swedenborg was not so naive as to think that all marriages are such marriages, and he knew that not everyone is able to find a marriage living up to these qualifications: "Separations take place after death because the unions on earth are seldom contracted from an inner sentiment of love, but only from an outer, which conceals the inner." [44]

Swedenborg's visions of married couples after death — though I'm not sure how to test or accept their veracity — are, at the very least, inspiring poetic imaginations of marriage. In one such vision, he discourses with a couple: "when the husband was speaking he spoke as if at the same time from his wife; and when the wife was speaking she spoke as if at the same time from her husband; for such was the union of minds whence the speech flows. Then I heard also the tone of

---

43 Emanuel Swedenborg, *The Delights of Wisdom Pertaining to Conjugal Love, after which Follow the Pleasures of Insanity Pertaining to Scortatory Love*, trans. Samuel M. Warren (New York, NY: Swedenborg Foundation, 1940), §41.
44 Ibid., §49.

voice of conjugal love, that it was inwardly simultaneous with, and also proceeding from, the delights of a state of peace and innocence."[45]

For Swedenborg, true Christian marriage makes manifest the marriage of Christ and the Church in a very real doctrine of correspondences: a correspondence represented in the conjugal act itself and the creation of a holy marriage. He does examine the perversity of soul that is the result of what he calls "scortatory" or unchaste love, but, as with all forms of sin, these are perversions of the good. But true marriage for him is nothing less than a *hieros gamos*: "For the man takes from the woman the beautiful blush of her love, and woman takes from man the shining luster of his wisdom, for the two spouses are united in soul and the abundance of their humanity appears in both."[46]

Swedenborg's intuitions concerning marriage in the afterlife beautifully affirm the Sacrament in a way that most theologies of marriage fail to do. In humanizing heaven, Swedenborg disrupts the tedious dichotomy between the spiritual and material that infects so much Christian thinking. As the great Polish poet Czeslaw Milosz observes, "Swedenborg, by humanizing God, supplied the makings of an anti-Hegelian vaccine."[47] Certainly a vaccine worth taking! In an age when the idea of marriage has been distorted and appropriated by the political, we are long past the time for a healthy reimagination of Christian marriage. The Eastern Orthodox theologian Jonathan Tobias articulates the corrective with profound grace: "The exclusiveness of marriage is not a limit, a temporary dispensation, or even a prophetic symbol whose identity will be subsumed by the eschaton. Rather, the 'exclusiveness' that chastity establishes, in cooperation with Grace, is a new body

---

45 Ibid., §42.
46 Ibid., §192.
47 Czeslaw Milosz, *The Land of Ulro*, trans. Louis Iribarne (New York, NY: Ferrar, Straus, Giroux, 1984), 160.

with an identity that will remain and grow ever in deification."[48] Truly a consummation devoutly to be wished.

From Russia with Love

It should come as no surprise that some of the most significant attempts in modern times to rehabilitate and reimagine sexuality in the context of Christian marriage have come from the Russian Sophiologists. With their profound attention to Things as They Are, in defiance of the spiritual-material split that was an outgrowth of nominalism and *natura pura*, the Russian Sophiologists quite organically followed what can only be called "spiritual common sense" in regards to sexuality and marriage.

Foremost among the Russian Sophiologists in his radical reassessment of love is Vladimir Solovyov who proceeds in his brief but monumental book *The Meaning of Love* to disclose the deep ontological significance of eros. First, Solovyov, rationally, phenomenologically, observes a fact of nature most might overlook: "the higher we ascend in the hierarchy of organisms, the weaker the power of propagation becomes, but, on the other hand, the greater the power of sexual attraction becomes."[49] As I tell my philosophy students, philosophy is more or less asking what seem to be stupid questions — but questions that, when taken into consideration, prove to be not very stupid at all. Such a question arises from Solovyov's observation: "Why does eros exist?" It doesn't seem to be a factor in the breeding habits of animals, yet it is the defining feature of human sexuality. Despite absurd Darwinist opinion that suggests "the biological imperative" is the *raison d'être* for sexual experience, this hardly inhabits the human imaginary when it comes to sex.

---

48   Jonathan Tobias, "The Persistence of Nuptial Union: Desire, Joy, and Spiritualization in Eternity," in *Jesus the Imagination, Volume II: The Being of Marriage* (Kettering, OH: Angelico Press, 2018): 7–12, at 8.
49   Vladimir Solovyov, *The Meaning of Love*, trans. Jane Marshall (1945), rev. and ed. Thomas R. Beyer, Jr. (Hudson, NY: Lindisfarne Press, 1985), 20.

As Julius Evola, following Solovyov, observes, "Reproduction is a possible outcome of sexual activity but is not in any way included in the actual experience of sexual excitement."[50] Just a cursory glance at the history of love poetry going back at least to the Song of Songs bears witness to this.

But Solovyov is not satisfied to stop here. In the often astonishing and refreshing way he approaches every subject, Solovyov brings radical insight to the question of eros. For Solovyov, eros is that which allows the individual to overcome him- or herself; it's the antidote to egoism:

> There is only one power which can from within undermine egoism at the root, and really does undermine it, namely love, and chiefly sexual love. . . . Recognizing in love the truth of another, not abstractly, but essentially, transferring in deed the center of our life beyond the limits of our empirical personality, we by so doing reveal and realize our own real truth, our own absolute significance, which consists just in our capacity to transcend our factual phenomenal being in our capacity to live not only in ourselves, but also in another.[51]

He even describes the phenomenon of love's effect on the lovers in terms to which Thomas and Rebecca Vaughan could give assent, as, "so to speak, a chemical union of two beings, of the same nature and of equal significance."[52]

For Solovyov, the importance of eros is not in the generation of a biological posterity (an idea that inhabits most papal encyclicals on the topic to some degree),[53] but as a triumph over death in a spiritual sense that at the same times *affirms* the sacredness of the flesh. "True spiritual love," he writes, "is

---

50 Julius Evola, *Eros and the Mysteries of Love: The Metaphysics of Sex*, trans. (1983; reprt. Rochester, VT: Inner Traditions, 1991), 14.
51 Vladimir Solovyov, *The Meaning of Love*, 45.
52 Ibid., 46.
53 Leo XIII, *Arcanum Divinae* (1880); Pius XI, *Casti connubii* (1930); and Paul VI, *Humanae vitae* (1968).

not a feeble imitation and anticipation of death, but a triumph over death. . . . False spirituality is a denial of the flesh; true spirituality is the regeneration of the flesh, its salvation, its resurrection from the dead."[54] Thomas and Rebecca Vaughan, it could be argued, were engaged in practical research in precisely such a project. Would that all the people of God were such prophets.

Another clear-thinking Russian radical, Nikolai Berdyaev, full of daring and lacking any fear of reprisal, boldly proclaimed a Sophiology of marriage that attends not only to the theology and philosophy of marriage but also takes into consideration its sociological aspects. Berdyaev's starting point is not, as is typical in contemporary religious polemic on the marriage question, to blame Darwin or secularization or "the culture." The culture he blames is Christian culture, engineered by celibates and monastics, who through a compromised anthropology long ago disfigured the nuptial image into one that privileged their own social contexts and power. "The sole purpose and justification of marriage," he writes, "was declared by Christianity to be procreation, dependent upon physical sexual intercourse, accompanied by loss of virginity. But it regarded this loss as a lower state and metaphysically despised it."[55] Thus began the long, slow decline to Freud, the Sexual Revolution, and Theodore McCarrick.

Berdyaev, a great lover of Boehme, naturally invokes the androgynous regeneration image of marriage that we have seen so many thinkers espousing an integral approach to marriage adopted. But Berdyaev, as a Russian Orthodox, unlike Cudworth, Swedenborg, and even Boehme, belonged to an ecclesial tradition in which marriage is still regarded as a sacrament. He criticizes the Church (and by this he implicates also the Catholic Church) for confusing and conflating the

---

54 Vladimir Solovyov, *The Meaning of Love*, 83.
55 Nicolas Berdyaev, *The Destiny of Man*, trans. Natalie Duddington (1955; reprt., New York, NY: Harper & Row, 1960), 241.

social and mystical meanings of marriage because he believes marriage is an ontological truth and not a political one. He doesn't mince words:

> Marriage and family which are not based upon love and freedom must be recognized as legal and economic institutions determined by law and social convention. They must be distinguished as a matter of principle from the sacrament of marriage and decisively pronounced to be neither sacred nor mystical in their significance. Only love, real love, one and eternal, that leads to the Kingdom of God, is sacred and mystical. It is a fact of a completely different order from the physiological life of sex and the social life of the family. And this mystical, sacred meaning of love has not been made manifest in the Church. . . . Conventional Christianity defends not the marriage, not the family, not the reality, but the form, the law, the marriage-rite. This is pure nominalism, a denial of ontological realities.[56]

In short, Berdyaev wants the tradition to own it. But, as with corporations and governments, the Church has followed a policy of "never complain, never explain" when it comes to the mistakes of the past which simply become subsumed into praxis without any relationship to reality or truth. "We've always done it this way." Christianity is haunted by a Gnostic disdain for the flesh, as much as it has struggled to overcome it. "We must get beyond the monastic and ascetic attitude which despised and hated the world, for it is incapable of comprehending the full truth of Christianity."[57]

Finally, Berdyaev, writing in the mid-1930s, faced with the rising specters of totalitarianism and fascism, like an Old Testament prophet called the Church to account for its sins:

---

56 Ibid., 235. My emphasis.
57 Nicolas Berdyaev, *Freedom and the Spirit*, trans. Olive Fielding Clarke (London: Geoffrey Bles/The Centenary Press, 1935), 265.

The judgment on Christianity is being passed in the sphere of sex and love and marriage. The prevailing Christian teaching denied the meaning of love and called it accursed. And thus it came about that love, not in a baser, but in a higher form, began to be affirmed outside of, and even against Christianity. The bourgeois family, with its economic egoism and exclusiveness, was sanctified, but the intimate life of love departed from Christianity. The higher meaning of love was revealed by the Provençal troubadours and defended in prose and poetry. In this connection, Christians lived in disagreement with dualism. Sex, love and marriage were bound up with the family, rather than with personality, and personality could not endure this state of affairs. One of the surprising things in history is the relentless severity of Christianity in the matter of love, and its unusual leniency toward property, which it has sanctioned in its most evil forms. [58]

He saw so clearly.

Berdyaev's friend and fellow expatriate Sergei Bulgakov also addressed marriage as a metaphysical reality in his work, though, as a theologian and a priest, he was not afforded the freedom his layman philosopher friend enjoyed. But, as in his Sophiology, he wasn't afraid to assert his individuality.

Bulgakov understands marriage in two ways, sacramentally and eschatologically. Sacramental marriage, the union of man and woman blessed by the Church, pacifies the tensions "between the spirit and flesh, between spiritual love and fleshly union . . . as the sacrificial path of communion and reproduction." [59] He distances himself, however, from the eschatological androgyny we have discussed, because for him the archetype for

---

58   Nicolas Berdyaev, *The Fate of Man in the Modern World*, trans. Donald A. Lowrie (1935; reprt., Ann Arbor, MI: University of Michigan / Ann Arbor Paperbacks, 1960), 124.
59   Sergius Bulgakov, *The Comforter*, trans. Boris Jakim (Grand Rapids, MI: William B. Eerdmanns Publishing Company, 2004), 331.

marriage is that found in both Song of Songs and Revelation, the referents to which, according to his interpretation, can only be Jesus and Mary, whose sexual identities are firmly fixed. He argues — against both Gregory of Nyssa and Boehme — that gender is not abolished at the Parousia: "Is it not evident that the Incarnation simultaneously eternalizes and certifies in their originality both the male gender, assumed by the Lord in His human nature, and the female gender, glorified and sanctified in the person of the Mother of God, who was resurrected and raised to heaven in Her flesh?"[60]

Bulgakov's attention never seems to be focused on the present moment, the present condition, but, rather, to eternal conditions either in prelapsarian Eden or at the Parousia. What occurs between is not as interesting to him; he always thinks in *spiritual principles*: "The male and the female in and of themselves, outside the fall, are in no way already *sex*, although afterwards they provide the foundations for the two sexual modes of human nature. Originally they are *spiritual* principles, some sort of spiritual qualifications."[61]

Bulgakov's defense of the integrity of gender difference and typology even after the Parousia is certainly commendable — and certainly correct — but, as we have seen with Cudworth, Swedenborg, and Tobias, there is no need to assume androgyny in a Christian sense means the obliteration of gender so much as it implies an integration in a way resonant with Jung's insights into the *coniunctio* as a psychological principle. The concept of the obliteration of gender is clearly harmful to psychological health and human flourishing, especially when it is interpreted medically or materialistically. But integration is another thing altogether.

---

60 Sergius Bulgakov, *The Bride of the Lamb*, trans. Boris Jakim (Grand Rapids, MI: William B. Eerdmanns Publishing Company, 2002), 441.
61 Sergius Bulgakov, *The Burning Bush: On the Orthodox Veneration of the Mother of God*, trans. Thomas Allan Smith (Grand Rapids, MI: William B. Eerdmanns Publishing Company, 2009), 82. Bulgakov's emphasis.

The Twentieth Century Dissolution

Beginning with Freud, whose pessimism infected all of his ideas, however brilliant, the twentieth century witnessed a steady and almost absolute dissolution of an integral understanding of marriage. This is primarily attributable to the almost pathological attention paid to sex and sexuality which jettisoned marriage to an ancillary position in the Positivist Grand Scheme of Things. The Sexual Revolution, indeed, celebrated sexuality as a right and denigrated marriage as an "institution," in the way that mental hospitals and prisons are institutions, and not as a paradigmatic structure of human flourishing encompassing all peoples of all nations throughout all of history. In a strange parallel to the belief in fairies or nature spirits (likewise held by all cultures until late modernity), marriage began more and more to be seen as anachronistic to a liberated and enlightened age. This trend was rendered all the more astonishing when marriage was asserted as a right to which gay and lesbian couples were entitled — a right to which no gay man or lesbian woman ever aspired until the concept's popularization in the early decades of the twenty-first century. It is clear that the desire for same-sex marriage was initially a response to prohibitive insurance and legal policies which barred same-sex partners from basic rights of companionship, inserting corporate caprices before the liberties of individual persons. In truth, in can be argued that such cruel-hearted policies created a desire for same-sex marriage and the legal rights pertaining to marriage. As a result, marriage in the cultural imaginary has been almost entirely secularized, with no spiritual or metaphysical correlative to be found.

During the twentieth century, however, some thinkers still maintained a metaphysical understanding of love and marriage, despite the onslaught of scientific materialism and psychoanalytical reductionism. Poet and novelist D. H. Lawrence, for example, attempted to reveal the spiritual dimensions of love disconnected from Christian morality, and he certainly makes a beautiful case for the spiritual reality of eros in human love. His poem "Gloire de Dijon," for example, may be one of the most beautiful love poems in the language, relying, as it does, on the simple act (which is never so simple) of description:

> When she rises in the morning
> I linger to watch her;
> She spreads the bath-cloth underneath the window
> And the sunbeams catch her
> Glistening white on the shoulders,
> While down her sides the mellow
> Golden shadow glows as
> She stoops to the sponge, and her swung breasts
> Sway like full-blown yellow
> Gloire de Dijon roses.
>
> She drips herself with water, and her shoulders
> Glisten as silver, they crumple up
> Like wet and falling roses, and I listen
> For the sluicing of their rain-dishevelled petals.
> In the window full of sunlight
> Concentrates her golden shadow
> Fold on fold, until it glows as
> Mellow as the glory roses.[62]

Unfortunately, Lawrence's prose psychological works are nowhere near as convincing as his poetry and fiction on the topic, but I have nothing but admiration for a man who dared to discover the essence of eros between a man and woman, even if disconnected from Christian metaphysics. At least he wasn't afraid.

On the other hand, Kenneth Rexroth, mentioned above, tried to combine Lawrence's erotic aesthetics with a metaphysical-religious sensibility. Unlike Lawrence, Rexroth maintained his Catholic faith, however idiosyncratically, over the span of his long life. For him, the Catholic Church was an environment

---

62 D. H. Lawrence, *Complete Poems*, ed. Vivian de Sola and Warren Roberts (New York, NY: Penguin, 1977).

more than an organization (though he had plenty to say about the organization) nowhere more itself than in its hospitality to mystics and "the anthropological, the folk religion, that engendered and nourished Western civilization."[63] Part of this ethos can be found in Rexroth's love poetry which evokes the mysticism of the Beguines, the eroticism of the Song of Songs, and a luminous attention to the Things of This World, all of which can be found in his poem, "The Phoenix and the Tortoise":

> I see in sudden total vision
> The substance of entranc'd Boehme's awe:
> The illimitable hour glass
> Of the universe eternally
> Turning, and the gold sands falling
> From God, and the silver sands rising
> From God, and the double-splendors of joy
> That fuse and divide again
> In the narrow passage of the Cross.
> . . . .
>
> My wife has been swimming in the breakers,
> She comes up the beach to meet me, nude,
> Sparkling with water, singing high and clear
> Against the surf. The sun crosses
> The hills and fills her hair, as it lights
> The moon and glorifies the sea
> And deep in the empty mountain melts
> The snow of winter and the glaciers
> Of ten thousand thousand years.[64]

It can only be regarded as tragedy that Rexroth's marriage ended painfully. Still, he has to be admired for attempting to maintain an integral understanding of marriage and eros during a most inhospitable century of pessimism.

Like these tragic figures, other twentieth-century thinkers and writers tried to maintain a religious-metaphysical

---

63   Kenneth Rexroth, *With Eye and Ear*, 91.
64   Kenneth Rexroth, *The Phoenix and the Tortoise*, 22 and 41.

sensibility regarding eros and marriage. Charles Williams, for example, tried to present what he called a "Romantic Theology" which restored eros to Christian thought on marriage.[65] Freud's protégé Wilhelm Reich, very interested in eros and its place in life, though ambivalent about marriage, nevertheless was attracted to the figure of Christ and the problematics of marriage and eros in Christian history and what he called "emotional plague."[66] And, finally, Alan Watts, an ordained priest of the Anglican Church, approached the subject and connected the conflicted relationship of Christianity to eros to a simultaneously conflicted relationship with nature: "The rift between God and nature would vanish if we knew how to experience nature, because what keeps them apart is not a difference of substance but a split in the mind."[67] Though all three had different approaches, different solutions, they had at least one thing in common: they knew something was wrong.

THE SOPHIOLOGICAL STRUCTURE OF MARRIAGE

The problem with defining marriage is that it includes a definition. What Augustine says of God is just as true of marriage: "Whatever you can fix upon, that is not it. Whatever you can comprehend by thought, that is not it."[68] We know (or think we know) what it is, but it deconstructs itself under our interrogation. There is a reason the Church calls the Sacraments "Mysteries," and in its ability to disclose its *mysterium* only in flashes the Nuptial Mystery reveals not only truths about the marital relationship but about human intercourse with God and with the Cosmos, and of God with the Cosmos.

---

65   See Charles Williams, *Outlines of a Romantic Theology*, ed. Alice Mary Hadfield (Beverly, CA: Apocryphile Press, 2005).

66   See Wilhelm Reich, *The Murder of Christ: The Emotional Plague of Mankind* (New York, NY: Farrar, Straus, and Giroux, 1953).

67   Alan W. Watts, *Nature, Man, and Woman* (New York, NY: Vintage Books, 1970), 189.

68   "Sermon 21 [on Psalm 53]"

This process needs must require a holding without grasping, a knowing without defining, a possession without purchase; for the truth of the *mysterion* is multivalent, holographic. What David Bohm and Basil Hiley have said about quantum mechanics can equally be applied to marriage (and all the Sacraments) in which we find "a new quality of *wholeness* of the entire system going beyond anything that can be specified solely in terms of the actual spatial relationships of all the particles."[69]

In its sacramental reality, marriage attests to *ontos*, "that which is." It affirms the primeval condition of existence: an existence that exists only in intimate relationship with an Other, an existence impossible without eros. We have seen various imaginations of this *ontos*. One is the mythos of united androgynous being, subsequently divided, then reunited in a more perfect form in Plato, Boehme, and the Kabbalah. The second Creation story of Genesis attests to this androgynous primeval condition before God takes a rib from the man and fashions a woman from it. This intersects with — and does not, it is important to note, negate — the imagination pronounced in Genesis's first Creation story and preferred by Bulgakov: "male and female created he them." Some commentators emphasize the first story, some the second, but they need to be read together, at the same time, holographically. They don't cancel each other out.

The *ontos* to which marriage witnesses figures the essential gesture of God which is then reflected in Creation and humanity, for, in the Anglican theologian A. M. Allchin's beautiful phrase, "The world is a wedding."[70] This wedding is always/already happening, was established at the Creation itself, and was sublimely articulated and completed when the Lord said to Sophia, "Let us make man in our image." Adam and Eve were never

---

69 D. Bohm and B. Hiley, *The Undivided Universe: An Ontological Interpretation of Quantum Theory* (London, UK: Routledge, 1993), 58. Emphasis in original.
70 A. M. Allchin, *The World Is a Wedding: Explorations in Christian Spirituality* (New York, NY: Oxford University Press, 1978).

married in an institutional sense: they were created married. Marriage, therefore, is a feature of Creation, a fact exquisitely illustrated in the sublime structure of the double helix.

Marriage is not only *ontos*; it is also *telos* and the aim of life, both *zoë* and *bios*. This is certainly implicit in the pseudo-Aristotelian dictum that what is first in thought is last in action, and characterizes so much of mystical and theological speculation regarding marriage. Even the biological imperative is able to be subsumed into this *telos*, which redeems it of its base scientific materialism and reveals the meaning of all existence. Pierre Teilhard de Chardin speaks directly to this in his concept of the Omega Point, the point in history and evolution in which all the Creation is divinized, united in Christ, "the star for which the world is waiting, without yet being able to give it a name, or rightly appreciate its true transcendence."[71] Teilhard correctly reads the presence of Sophia, she who attended the Lord at the Creation (Proverbs 8), in this trajectory accompanying all creatures great and small on the journey to the wedding.

As *telos*, then, marriage is also *eschaton*. Bulgakov emphasized this aspect of marriage at the expense of marriage in the present, as if he were always living in the future. But the wedding is always/already happening. In eternity, there is no time, so the marriage of Christ and the Church, prophesied in Revelation is already a reality. In fact, it may be better to say that it is not we who approach the *eschaton* but the *eschaton* that approaches us. Quantum theory suggests that time exists but in our perception, but our presence (*parousia*) or lack of it conditions whether or not the wedding is present as present, both awareness and gift. Indeed, there is something of David Bohm's notion of implicate order at work here: Christian marriage is implicit in the *eschaton* and the *eschaton* is implicit in Christian marriage. The world is a wedding.

---

71   Pierre Teilhard de Chardin, *The Divine Milieu: An Essay on the Interior Life* (New York, NY: Harper & Row, Publishers, 1960), 137.

These things all inform Christian marriage, though all too often they are obscured by fallenness, brokenness, and sorrow. Nevertheless, the spiritual potential in the eros proper to Christian marriage can effect a transaction informed by the eschatological marriage. We find an apt description in John Donne's "The Extasie":

> This Extasie doth unperplex
>   (We said) and tell us what we love;
> Wee see by this, it was not sexe,
>   Wee see, we saw not what did move;
>
> But as all severall soules containe
>   Mixture of things, they know not what,
> Love, these mixt soules doth mixe againe,
>   And makes both one, each this and that. [72]

For this extasie *doth* unperlpex, as it restores wholeness not only to the man and woman so united, but to the universe.

The arrival at a mystical marriage, however, does not come without effort. We all have our own struggles to overcome, and in marriage these struggles are multiplied as now the two have become one flesh. Our own unregenerated experiences and psychological conditioning seek their revenges upon us the closer we come to the sacred precincts of love. This may be why marriage is often called a kind of martyrdom by the Church. Nevertheless, we are truly speaking of a journey of souls here, and the alchemical processes by which the mystical and chymical wedding is achieved. I find the great faerie ballad "Tam Lin" particularly helpful and instructive for outlining this process.

In the tale, a young woman (named Janet or Margaret according to different versions of the ballad) finds herself with child by her beloved, Tam Lin, a knight who has been enthralled by the Queen of Faeries. In her attempt to deliver him from the Faerie Queen, Tam Lin tells her what marvels to expect:

---

72 *The Complete Poetry of John Donne*, ed. John T. Shawcross (Garden City, NY: Anchor Books, 1967), lines 29–36.

First they'll change me in your arms
Into some esk or adder.
Hold me close and fear me not,
For I am your baby's father.

Then they'll turn me in your arms
Into a lion wild.
Hold me tight and fear me not
As you would hold your child.

Then they'll turn me in your arms
Into a red-hot bar of iron.
Hold me close and fear me not,
For I will do no harm.

Then they'll turn me in your arms
Into some burning lead.
Throw me into well-water
And throw me in with speed.

Last they'll turn me in your arms
Into a naked knight.
Wrap me up in your green mantle,
And keep me out of sight.

In my experience, these myriad transformations accurately portray, in symbolic form, the kinds of transformations through which married couples process on their way to the mystical marriage. The key refrain, "Hold me close and fear me not," may, indeed, be the best piece of marital advice one might impart to the newlywed. For marriage, among its many mysteries, is a process of humanizing the remnants of instinct and bringing the light of healing to damaged psychologies.

This is why Jung's intuitions (not to say conclusions) about the *coniunctio oppositorum* are so important. He knew that only by the reintegration of male and female in the psyche but also in ontology can human flourishing be accomplished. This is not an exchange that can transpire through medical or surgical interventions or via a political act. The wedding is not a mechanical problem, not a cosmetic procedure, and not a legal intervention. It is not something constructed. It can only be realized through intimacy with the other, the opposite, the absolutely other: through the chymical wedding, *the hieros gamos*, the divine marriage. The world is a wedding, and every wedding is a world.

3

Creation I

THE FATE OF THE TREE

For he hath given me the true knowledge of the things
that are: to know the disposition of the whole world, and
the virtues of the elements. . . . The natures of living
creatures, and rage of wild beasts, the force of winds,
and reasonings of men, the diversities of plants, and
the virtues of roots, And all such things as are hid and
not foreseen, I have learned: for Wisdom, which is the
fashioner of all things, taught me.

~: Wisdom 7 : 17, 20 – 21

Now the green blade riseth from the buried grain,
Wheat that in the dark earth many days hath lain.
Love lives again, that with the dead hath been.
Love is come again like wheat that springeth green.

~: Anglican hymn

BREEZE BLOWS LIGHTLY FROM THE
west this morning, though it's still cold. Two days ago
sixty-mile-an-hour winds toppled a hundred-year-old
white pine that, in its fall, just missed both the chicken coop
and the apiary, a solitary twig brushing the side of just one
hive all that was left to file on a damage report. But now I sit
here, waiting, in a blind made of sticks and branches to see if
the deer will come.

Just after eight o'clock, I hear movement in the swamp before
me and turn off the safety of my double-barrel sixteen-gauge.
Then, almost as if materializing from an invisible world, the
antlers and head of a buck appear from among the sumac and

alder. And then he presents himself to me. I'm a good shot, but my hands tremble as I take aim, adrenaline combining with my morning coffee's burst of caffeine, so I need to take a couple of breaths to calm myself. Calmed, I shoot. The buck reels, bolts, and I wait for twenty minutes before calling my two youngest sons from the house to help me track it. My ten-year-old son Daniel finds it in a field about forty yards from the blind. We'll eat the heart for lunch and will butcher the deer after it's hung to age in the cold barn for five days. Later this evening, I will give a lecture on Sophiology and the Metaphysical Poets at nearby Hillsdale College. It's a good day.

Later, my friend Therese Schroeder-Sheker calls me to talk about other things, but I tell her about the deer and its almost miraculous appearance from out of the swamp. Most of my scholarly and intellectual friends don't like to talk about such things, preferring, it seems, to outsource the killing that sustains their lives (and, sorry, but plants are also killed for food). But Therese — who, like me is from Detroit — has lived in Colorado, Montana, and Oregon, so she's been around hunting and game for a goodly portion of her adult life. She tells me something she heard from a Native American medicine man. "Michael," she says, "you didn't find the deer: it gave itself to you." I know this to be true.

Therese is a musician, but poets also have a sensitivity to these things. Robert Kelly, for example, describes such an encounter in his prose poem "The Heavenly Country":

> At night it was almost cold, so we slept with blankets
> or walked out in sweaters early morning to see deer or
> whatever else might reveal itself to us. That it is a matter
> of It willing to reveal to Us I have never doubted. [1]

I didn't always hunt, though I come from French voyageur stock on my father's side: men who came to the new found land

---

1   Robert Kelley, *The Convections* (Santa Barbara, CA: Black Swallow Press, 1978), 63.

in order that, among other things, they could hunt without fear of reprisal, a privilege only afforded the nobility in the Old World. I grew up around hunting and guns, but in my late teens and twenties fancied myself more spiritually evolved than my parents (an affliction particular to modernity) and practiced vegetarianism for about a decade. I was, I regret to say, sick much of the time. When my wife was pregnant with our eldest child she craved liverwurst and I dreamt of hunting. Our bodies and souls were telling us it was time for a change in diet.

Even though I am a biodynamic farmer, the hunt embeds me in nature even more than the life of cultivation and animal husbandry. It reaffirms my role as a part of Creation. Farming does, too, in its way, but hunting connects us to the wild in a manner quite a bit different from that of the cycle of planting. Gary Snyder captures something very true about this in his poem "Long Hair":

> Once every year, the Deer catch human beings. They
> do various things which irresistibly draw men near them;
> each one selects a certain man. The Deer shoots the man,
> who is then compelled to skin it and carry its meat home
> and eat it. Then the deer is inside the man. He waits and
> hides in there, but the man doesn't know it. When
> enough Deer have occupied enough men, they will strike all
> at once. The men who don't have Deer in them will
> also be taken by surprise, and everything will change some.
> This is called "takeover from inside."[2]

Hunting, then, is a very primitive (in the best sense of the word) spiritual activity and "submerges man deliberately in that formidable mystery and therefore contains something of religious rite and emotion in which homage is paid to what is divine, transcendent, in the laws of Nature."[3] Our hidden

---

2 Gary Snyder, *The Gary Snyder Reader: Poetry, Prose, and Translations, 1952–1998* (Ann Arbor, MI: Counterpoint, 1999), 462.
3 José Ortega y Gasset, *Meditations on Hunting*, trans. Howard B. Wescott (New York: Charles Scribner's Sons, 1972), 98.

wildness discloses itself in this most primal of ontological structures.

It is in farming, though, that my connection to nature is most consistently nurtured and cultivated. Indeed, sometimes I wonder if I'm cultivating the farm or the farm is cultivating me. I'm so immersed in this reciprocity that the distinctions are not always very clear.

Farming, like most things, is a life of rhythms: of day and night and their expansion and contraction over the year; of the year itself; of the traces of the sun, moon, and planets; of the waking and sleeping of the farm as a being. Each farm, each garden, possesses its own being: it has its own personality, its own character, its own qualities, its own relationships. The farmer recognizes this being and tries to find ways for it to flourish. This is not a dialectic of mastery.

My relationship to farming started with gardens. Growing up in Detroit, farming was not a feature of my experience, but I was fascinated with gardens and with vegetable gardens in particular. My parents never had a vegetable garden, though my mother would plant flats of moss roses, petunias, and snap dragons every summer. Our next door neighbor, Mr. Blackley, a Scottish immigrant, kept a victory garden behind his garage, so I would look at it over the chain-link fence in absolute wonder. In the spring when I would go to the grocery store with my mother as a five- or six-year-old, I would ask her if I could look at the packages of vegetable seeds in their display rack. She could have left me there for hours if she'd wanted. The colorful images of carrots, beets, and cabbage, of radishes, onions, and lettuces thrilled me and filled my imagination as much as any picture-book. I even talked my father into digging me out a small plot — it couldn't have been more than two feet by three — where I sprinkled some carrot and radish seed. I didn't know how to care for it — nobody told me what to do — so weeds and grass took over. Nevertheless, I did manage to pull out at least one carrot. Magic.

It was not until my mid-twenties that I returned to the idea of a garden, no doubt because I had my own house and a yard at that point. Eventually, my interest turned into an obsession, then a preoccupation, then an occupation. I studied Rudolf Steiner's agriculture lectures and had a supportive group of friends also interested in farming and gardening biodynamically. One, a lanky Texan named Mike, who had worked with biodynamic pioneer Alan York, taught me the ropes of double-digging, composting, and tree pruning — for which he deserves heaven if I have anything to say in the matter. I undertook to make all of the biodynamic preparations I could while living in a rental in Ferndale, Michigan. How odd the UPS driver must have thought it was to deliver packages of sheep skulls, cow horns, and stag bladders to my door. But I wanted to know how to *do it*. Theory is one thing, practice another.

Biodynamic farming reinforces the very Christian, very Catholic notion of the sacredness of the year. The agricultural cycle and the liturgical cycle are (or used to be) beautifully intertwined. Much like in Celtic knotwork, to remove one of these strands from life is to destroy life's integral unity and beauty. Unfortunately, that is precisely what happened over the course of the centuries until now we find Christianity and agriculture estranged from each other, to the detriment of both. What we have instead are utilitarian liturgical and agricultural models that have even succeeded in making human beings strangers to the food they eat, to the foundations of religion, to the cosmos, and to each other — all relationships that used to be assumed.

This has not always been the case, and a belief in the sacred coalescence of religion and agriculture is not even particular to Christianity. In Virgil's *Georgics*, for example, the great Augustan poet reminds the reader of the proper disposition to the land and the gods:

> Mark the months and signs of heaven; whither Saturn's
> cold star withdraws itself into what circles of the sky

strays the Cyllenian fire. Above all, worship the gods, and pay great Ceres her yearly rites, sacrificing on the glad sward, with the setting of winter's last days, when clear springtime is now come. Then are lambs fat and wine is most mellow; then sweet is sleep, and thick are the shadows on the hills. Then let all your country folk worship Ceres; for her wash the honeycomb with milk and soft wine, and three times let the luck-bringing victim pass round the young crops, while the whole crowd of your comrades follow exulting, and loudly call Ceres into their homes; nor let any put his sickle to the ripe corn, ere for Ceres he crown his brows with oaken wreath, dance artless measures, and chant her hymns. [4]

Examples of how Christianity was once entwined with agricultural are often dismissed with charges of "paganism," the go-to libel for lazy Puritans, whether Protestant, Catholic, or secularist. But even a cursory knowledge of how the liturgical cycle when imbued with folk customs enriched human life clearly indicates how impoverished we are. A world without the blessing of the fields, St. John's fires, and Lammas bread is a shadow world, indeed. H. J. Massingham describes this tragedy as one demarcated by "the dividing line when Christendom began to depart from Christianity." Can it be described any other way? His diagnosis is irrefutable: "Nor can the Christian Faith (seeing that there is no alternative to it) itself be rejuvenated unless it be equally shown that its own division from nature has pauperized it as an all-sufficient gospel for modern, grown-up, Western man, wrecked in the bitter sea of his own self-will." [5]

What is easy to miss in (re)connecting the liturgical with the agricultural is that what we are really talking about is a regeneration of Creation. Liturgical acts, sacramental acts,

---

4   Virgil, *Georgics* 1.335–50. In Virgil, *Eclogues, Georgics, Aeneid I–VI*, trans. H. Rushton Fairclough, rev. ed. (Cambridge, MA: Loeb Classical Library, 1956), 105.

5   H. J. Massingham, *The Tree of Life* (London: Chapman & Hall, 1943), 17.

and agricultural acts *should be* (and rarely are, unfortunately)
deeds reaffirming, reconsecrating, and regenerating Creation.
So much the less when they are estranged from each other. The
marriage of folk and liturgical customs found in the practices
of the medieval peasantry maintained this understanding in
the agricultural setting, but even earlier practices maintained
it with Creation in its wilder forms. The Celtic churches, so
difficult to perceive clearly through the mists of history, moved
in such an awareness. The legends of the Celtic saints — Patrick,
Brendan, Brigit, and Columba for example — are rich with a
natural world barely touched by agriculture. It is also interesting to note that Celtic monasticism with its extraordinary
emphasis on asceticism and learning arose in a geographical area
almost complete devoid of urban centers. It may be precisely
because of this that Celtic monks participated in the wildness
of Creation in a manner almost entirely unknown in other
contexts. The exquisite Welsh "Litany of the Creation" (c. 7th
century) voices this beautifully:

> I beseech the people of heaven with bright-armed Michael;
> I beseech you by the triad of wind, sun, and moon.
> I beseech you by water and the cruel air;
> I beseech you by fire, I beseech you by earth. [6]

It is no accident, I think, that the alternate title for St. Patrick's
extraordinary "Breastplate" is "The Deer's Cry."

My own path into farming — and deeper into Christianity — was accompanied by the intuition (that is the only word
for it) of the inner (and real) meaning of the Creation. In my
twenties I had heard from a friend that Rudolf Steiner once
said that there were three meetings people have with the Trinity
over their lives. In the daily rhythm of sleeping and waking,
Steiner said, we meet the Holy Spirit via our guardian angel
in the deepest part of sleep. Over the course of our lives, he

---

6   Oliver Davies, trans. with Thomas O'Loughlin, *Celtic Spirituality* (New
York: Paulist Press, 1999), 298.

continued, we meet "the Father Principle," but not before the twenty-ninth year (the cycle of Saturn). But over the course of a year, by paying attention to the subtle changes in Nature day by day and as mirroring the liturgical year, we meet the Son. For Steiner, Christ united himself with the earth through his incarnation, baptism, and, especially, crucifixion and resurrection, so it would make sense that we could learn to know Christ through attending to the rhythms of the year, both liturgical and cosmic. "When the year's course is again felt by humanity as an inner connection with the Mystery of Golgotha, then, by attuning the feelings of the soul with both the course of the year and the secret of the Mystery of Golgotha, a true social feeling will be the true solution, or at any rate the true continuation of what is today so foolishly called . . . the social question."[7] I didn't know whether or not this was true, but I figured it was at least worth exploring. Over thirty years later, I still haven't stopped this exploration. If we can meet Christ through Nature, he is available to anyone paying attention to the Creation. This is the real takeover from inside.

Farming, then, working with the earth and its rhythms, is in its ideal form to also work with Christ, a truly sacred vocation. Unfortunately, so much of what goes by the name of farming these days — even, alas, in much allegedly "organic" farming — is oblivious, if not antithetical, to such an ethos. But the reality of the Crucifixion enlivened a dying earth with spiritual forces: it's as simple as that. Sergei Bulgakov explains the phenomenon with luminous power:

> The spear wound, not the breaking of His bones, is the conclusion of Christ's salvific sacrifice for the redemption of humankind. This blood and water wash human sin and create the New Testament Church, with its grace-bestowing mysterious gifts: baptismal water and eucharistic blood. Out of the side of the old Adam was

---

7   Rudolf Steiner, *Cosmic and Human Metamorphoses*, trans. (Blauvelt, NY: Garber Communications, 1989), 67.

created woman, who tempted him to fall. But the wound delivered to humankind from Adam's side is healed by the spear wound in Jesus's side. The blood and water that flowed into the world abide in the world. They sanctify this world as the pledge of its future transfiguration. Through the precious streams of Christ's blood and water that flowed out of His side, all creation was sanctified — heaven and earth, our earthly world, and all the stellar worlds. [8]

Given this reality, the methods of conventional farming, with its reliance on chemical fertilizers, insecticides, and herbicides — a true culture of death — and its promotion of GMOs and the spreading prohibitions against saving seed, amount to sacrilege. To engage in it is to trample on the image of Christ.

It might be suggested that I am simply projecting my own ecological concerns, my own biodynamic biases, onto a religion that is responsible for subduing and enslaving nature, and thereby guilty of all the ills of conquest and colonialism according to a very jaundiced reading of God's command to Adam and Eve in Genesis 1:28: "Be fruitful and increase in number; fill the earth and subdue it." Not so fast. As Margaret Barker observes, the Hebrew word usually translated as "subdue," *kbš*, more properly means "bind," therefore implying that Adam was bound to Creation by way of a *covenant*. As such, "Adam was to maintain the bonds of creation." [9] So it should be no surprise that theologians as diverse as Jürgen Moltmann and Pierre Teilhard de Chardin have likewise discovered the Mystery of Christ at the center of Creation. "If the creative God himself dwells in his creation," writes Moltmann, "then he is making it his own home, 'on earth as it is in heaven.' All created beings then find in nearness to him the inexhaustible

---

8 Sergius Bulgakov, *The Holy Grail and the Eucharist*, trans. and ed. Boris Jakim (Hudson, NY: Lindisfarne Books, 1997), 33. My emphasis.
9 Margaret Barker, *Creation: A Biblical Vision for the Environment* (London: T & T Clark, 2010), 122.

wellspring of their life, and for their part find home and rest in God."[10] Teilhard turns to the story of Jacob's ladder to help us see this reality: "As Jacob said, awakening from his dream, the world, this palpable world, to which we brought boredom and callousness reserved for profane places, is in truth a holy place, and we did not know it."[11] The *Shepherd of Hermas*, written in the second century, likewise attests to this: "'Listen,' said [the angel], 'the name of the Son of God is great and incomprehensible and supports the entire cosmos.'"[12] I am hardly proposing an innovation.

The image of Jacob's ladder, in fact, bears archetypal significance for this journey. Anyone attentive or sensitive to the Creation — to the properties of plants and stones, the habits of animals, the tilth of the soil, the movements of the star and planets — will by degrees come to an intuition of its verity. The Paracelsian physician and Metaphysical poet Henry Vaughan was such a person. The seventeenth-century poet's *oeuvre*, with its synthesis of the natural and spiritual worlds so foreign to most of his poetic contemporaries, speaks directly to the idea that all things in Creation hold the capacity to reveal the Divine. As such, he alludes to Jacob's ladder at least five times in his masterwork, *Silex Scintillans* (1650 and 1655); it is a central motif for him. "Regeneration," the inaugural poem of the collection, sets the tone:

> With that, some cryed, *Away*; straight I
> > Obey'd, and led
> Full East, a faire, fresh field could spy
> > Some call'd it, *Jacobs Bed*;
> > A Virgin-soile, which no
> > > Rude feet ere trod,

---

10   Jürgen Moltmann, *God in Creation: A New Theology of Creation and the Spirit of God*, The Gifford Lectures 1984–1985, trans. Margaret Kohl (San Francisco: Harper & Row, 1985), 5.

11   Pierre Teilhard de Chardin, *The Divine Milieu: An Essay on the Interior Life* (New York: Harper & Row, 1960), 89.

12   Parable 9.14.5.

Where (since he stept there,) only go
    Prophets, and friends of God. (lines 25 – 32)

This sets the stage for vision, insight into the workings of
nature and of God. But these rewards, Vaughan knows, are
inseparable from *struggling* or *contending* with not only God
but oneself. He phrases this sensibility in "Rules and Lessons":

Serve God before the world; let him not go
Until thou hast a blessing, then resigne
The whole unto him; and remember who
Prevail'd by *wrestling* ere the *Sun* did *shine*.
    Poure *Oyle* upon the *stones*, weep for thy sin,
    Then journey on, and have an eie to heav'n.

                                    (lines 19 – 24)

Notice how, in Vaughan (not to mention Genesis), the polarities
between stone (or matter) and light (the shining, heaven) live in
mutual communication, a dynamic made all the more evident in
his selected title for his work: *Silex Scintillans*, "the sparking flint."

Jacob named the site of his vision *Beth-El*, "the House of God,"
and there is no reason to believe that every parcel of Creation
is not a potential *Bethel*. Indeed, religious experiences tied to
nature are too numerous to count, almost universal in their
distribution. I would wager that they are among the most common of human experiences, though many if not most people
lack a sufficient language for describing their experiences. Joan
of Arc's initial visionary experiences, for example, occurred at
what was known as "The Ladies' Tree" or "The Faeries' Tree" in
her village of Domremy. Some villagers even claimed to have
seen fairies there, but Joan only claimed to have seen saints
Catherine and Margaret and the Archangel Michael who "was
not alone, but was accompanied by angels from heaven."[13]
Even the then-hardened Marxist economist Sergei Bulgakov

---

13   W. S. Scott, trans. and ed., *The Trial of Joan of Arc, Being a Verbatim
Report of the Proceedings from the Orleans Manuscript* (Westport, CT: Associated
Booksellers, 1956), 78.

was not impervious to the glory shining through the landscape one sunset while traveling through the Caucasus:

> I started to wonder what would happen if the cosmos were not a desert and its beauty not a mask of deception — if nature were not death, but life. If he existed, the merciful and loving Father, if nature was the vesture of his love and glory, and if the pious feelings of my childhood, when I used to live in his presence, when I loved him and trembled because I was weak, were true, then the tears and inspiration of my adolescence, the sweetness of my prayers, my innocence, and all those emotions which I had rejected and trodden down would be vindicated, and my present outlook with its emptiness and deadness would appear nothing more than blindness and lies, and what a transformation it would bring to me![14]

But the Glory of the Lord doesn't only shine through the beauties of nature. Bernadette Soubirous' first vision of the Virgin Mary came in a small alcove near a garbage dump, and Jacob Boehme's insight into the nature of God occurred through the reflection of light off a pewter dish. There is no place where grace cannot appear. Beth-El: you are here.

But you are also not here.

One thing that keeps us from the experience of the Real is our pathological drive to control everything from fertility, to illness, to our environments. We regulate fertility through artificial birth control, through abortion, through "waiting until we've established our careers." Fertility terrifies us, so we treat it as a disease, even, in some cases, by comparing a growing fetus to a parasite. It terrifies us so much that fertility rates have been plummeting for decades while NGOs have been advocating for a massive population decrease. If we learned

---

14 Sergius Bulgakov, *A Bulgakov Anthology: Sergius Bulgakov 1871–1944*, trans. Natalie Duddington and James Pain, ed. James Pain and Nicolas Zernov (London: SPCK, 1976), 10–11.

anything through the COVID-19 panic, it has to be that people have fetishized antiseptic living into a demigod. When people used to get the flu, it was just one of those things. You took some over-the-counter medication or homeopathy and let the illness run its course. After COVID, illness somehow became evidence of moral turpitude and selfishness. Another thing we learned is that it is "safer" to encounter others through virtual environments, like Zoom, rather than by interacting, by exchanging genetic information, in the face-to-face communion of a lived life. This is entirely neurotic.

These phenomena are merely symptomatic of a way of life (*bios*) completely divorced from Life (*zoë*). We live lives in which, as John Donne says, "'Tis all in pieces, all coherence gone,"[15] divorced as we are from the world of clouds, of plants, of animals, and from each other, from the cosmos, and, because of these, from God. Indeed, the inverse is also true: we are distanced from the world of clouds, plants, and animals because we are distanced from God. The integral unity of life and purpose that we instinctively feel lacking is really a product of our disengagement from the calendar, and by this I mean both the calendar of the seasons and the liturgical calendar, both of which reflected each other once upon a time. 1 Enoch is very clear about the repercussions of our disconnect from the cosmos and God:

> And in those days the angel Uriel answered and said to me: "Behold, I have shown thee everything, Enoch, and I have revealed everything to thee that thou shouldst see this sun and this moon, and the leaders of the stars of the heaven and all those who turn them, their tasks and times and departures.
>
> "And in the days of the sinners the years shall be shortened, And their seed shall be tardy on their lands and fields, And all things on the earth shall alter, And shall not appear in their time: And the rain shall be kept back

---

15 "An Anatomie of the World," line 213.

and the heaven shall withhold [it]. And in those times
the fruits of the earth shall be backward, and shall not
grow in their time, and the fruits of the trees shall be
withheld in their time. And the moon shall alter her
order, and not appear at her time." [16]

Surrounded by the scientific hubris that seeks to "improve"
seed by genetic engineering and that attempts to dim the sun,
the moon, and stars through the dispersal of calcium car-
bonate through the atmosphere (among many other foolish
ideas) — things we have let happen through either ignorance
or inertia — is it any wonder that our impact on the Creation grows more and more devastating? We operate, not in a
cooperative manner with nature, but according to a paradigm
characterized by suppression, dominance, and control, but
above all by hubris. We shouldn't ask why wildfires, droughts,
and devastating hurricanes occur so often, we should ask why
they don't happen more.

The reason for this is that the world has a soul, the *anima
mundi*. This is an idea found throughout history. Plato, in the
Timaeus, describes it this way: "we may say that the world
came into being — a living creature truly endowed with soul
and intelligence by the providence of God." [17] And because the
world is a living creature endowed with soul, all things within
it participate in this life. As Plotinus writes, "the work of soul
is something awake, both that within it and in the same way
that which goes out to something else. Soul therefore makes
alive all the other things which do not live of themselves, and
makes them live the sort of life by which it lives itself." [18] The
Judeo-Christian tradition has a proper name for the bearer of
this soul: "Wisdom, the fashioner of all things" (Wisdom 7:22).

---

16 80:1–5.

17 *Timaeus* 30c. Trans. Benjamin Jowett, from *The Collected Dialogues of
Plato, Including the Letters*, ed. Edith Hamilton and Huntington Cairns (New
York: Bollingen, 1961).

18 *Ennead* 4.3.36–38. From *Enneads* IV. 1–9, trans. A. H. Armstrong
(Cambridge, MA: Loeb Classical Library, 1984).

To live in accord with Wisdom is to live in accord with both Creation and God. The poetic metaphysics of this understanding can be found, among others, in the symbolism of the *harmonia mundi* and of the tree.

The *harmonia mundi*, literally "harmonies of the world" but often referred to as "the Music of the Spheres," has a rich history in the West, probably stemming from Pythagoras and alluded to by Plato in the *Timaeus*. Plotinus provides a very beautiful description:

> The harmonious adjustment of the souls to the order of this All of ours witnesses to this: they are not cut off from it, but fit themselves in in their descents and make one harmony with its circuit, so that their fortunes and their lives and their choices are indicated by the figures made by the heavenly bodies and they sing, as it were, with one voice and are never out of tune. (And this is more properly the hidden meaning of the doctrine that the heavenly spheres move musically and melodically.) [19]

Many Renaissance writers and thinkers touched on the idea: Robert Fludd and Johannes Kepler, for example, and Shakespeare in his play *Pericles, Prince of Tyre*. It is a very simple concept: to live in harmony with Creation and God is to be at one with All That Is. Conversely, to be out of harmony with Creation and God is to invite corruption, infertility, and desolation upon the world and, as we are part of the world, ourselves.

The image of the tree, as the Tree of Life, may be the symbol *par excellence* of Wisdom from antiquity. The Tree, of course, makes its first appearance in Genesis, but it was also a feature of First Temple Judaism as an icon of Wisdom before Her worship was banned under the reforms of Josiah and her devotees driven into exile. The Tree returns in Revelation at the Restoration of All Things: "And he showed me a river of water of life, clear as

---

19   *Enneads* 4.3.20 – 29.

crystal, proceeding from the throne of God and of the Lamb. In the midst of the street thereof, and on both sides of the river, was the tree of life, bearing twelve fruits, yielding its fruits every month, and the leaves of the tree were for the healing of the nations" (22:1-2). Margaret Barker reads this restoration as the restoration of Wisdom, the Divine Sophia, to her proper place in Christian worship and understanding. For her, "The fate of the tree [is] the fate of Wisdom," which is why she argues that the earliest Christian communities understood it in precisely this way: "When John saw the woman and the tree in the holy of holies [i.e., Revelation 22], he showed that the Christians were faithful to the older ways. Their temple was the ancient temple, and so the woman and her tree and everything they represented shaped their way of thinking. Wisdom/Miriam was the mother of the Messiah, and that is how the Christians told the story of the birth of Jesus."[20]

This is the challenge presented to us at this point in history. We find ourselves confronted with a choice between the Real or a simulacrum of the Real, what the Kabbalah calls the *qlipoth*, the world of demonic powers.[21] Do we assist in the work of salvation by recognizing Sophia's place in Creation, thereby calling her out of exile? Or do we follow the trajectory of death that has and will continue to wreak havoc on Creation and on our own souls as they descend into the technological and technocratic abyss of the *qlipoth*? Too often, Christians, or any people of good will, leave the work of salvation to politicians or to an amorphous future event, the Coming of the Messiah. But our actions constitute a call, a summons. As Nikolai Berdyaev so stridently says, "My salvation is bound up with that not only of other men but also of animals, plants, minerals, of every blade of grass — all must be transfigured and brought into the Kingdom of God. And this depends upon

---

20　Margaret Barker, *Creation*, 266, 265.
21　Gershom Scholem, *On the Kabbalah and Its Symbolism*, trans. Ralph Manheim (London: Routledge and Kegan Paul, 1965), 114.

my creative efforts."[22] Salvation, that is, is not a spectator sport.

Francis of Assisi understood this better than anyone. He ends his beautiful *Canticle of the Sun* with a panacea for those lost in the qlipotic wasteland: "O Creatures all! Praise and bless my Lord, and be grateful! / Serve Him with deep humility." All the Kingdoms of Creation participate in the Glory of the Lord, even Sister Bodily Death. The Life that informs all life does not vanish with our seeming disappearance from view. He becomes even more real to us. The cosmos, to echo Bulgakov, is not a desert and its beauty is not a mask of deception. Creation is not death, but life. And, for the Christian, even death is not death, but part of Creation, though we look into a glass darkly. For we move from glory to Glory, from life to Life.

> And if you ask a farmer, however old, for whom he is planting, he will unhesitatingly reply, "For the immortal gods, who have willed not only that I should receive these blessings from my ancestors, but also that I should hand them on to posterity."
>
> ~:Cicero[23]

---

22   Nicolas Berdyaev, *The Destiny of Man*, trans. Natalie Duddington (New York: Harper & Row, 1960), 294.

23   *De senectute* 7.23. From Cicero, *De senectute, De amicitia, De divinatione*, trans. William Armistead Falconer (London: Heinemann, 1923), 33.

4
Creation II
THE INVENTION OF HONEY

ARL KERÉNYI'S 1976 BOOK DIONYSOS: *Archetypal Image of Indestructible Life* is one of the more fascinating works in my library. Since the first time I read Euripides' *The Bacchae* over thirty years ago, followed by readings of *Frogs*, Aristophanes' great work of combined literary criticism and slapstick (a combination so much in need today!), and Friedrich Nietzsche's powerful *The Birth of Tragedy*, the figure of Dionysos has—true to form—possessed me. But Kerényi's book deepened this attraction in ways I couldn't have anticipated.

Primary among the reasons for my appreciation for Kerényi's exposition on Dionysos is his discussion of the god's relationship to honey. Now, I'm a beekeeper, so anything about bees — such as the fourth book of Virgil's *Georgics* — interests me, and the history of beekeeping is a long one rich with mythic imagination. Drawing on the vast mythological treasure troves of antiquity, Kerényi offers a description of the god's attributes, full of splendor:

> He was said to have invented honey, and the ground on which his handmaidens, the maenads, danced was said to have flowed with milk, wine, and the "nectar of bees." It was also said that honey dripped from the thyrsos staffs that the maenads carried. Before the feeding of the infant Dionysos, a privilege of his non-animal, sacred nurses, his lips were sprinkled with honey. [1]

---

1 Carl Kerényi, *Dionysos: Archetype of Indestructible Life*, trans. Ralph Manheim (Princeton: Princeton University Press, 1976), 31.

Euripides' account bears a bit more of chthonic strangeness:

> All crowned themselves with ivy, oak, and flowering
> vines. One took her thyrsus, struck a rock,
> and water leapt out, pure as dew.
> Another set her staff in solid ground
> and the god sent her a fountain of wine.
> If anyone was thirsty for a drink of milk
> she scrabbled her sharp fingers in the earth
> and it came out spurting white. Sweet streams of honey
> too came dripping from the ivy-covered wands. [2]

Later in the text, Kerényi traces the honey-Dionysos connection to the making of mead, which existed in Greece long before the introduction of the vine.

Mead is a very easy alcoholic beverage to make. I make upwards of twenty gallons or so every year: metheglins (flavored with herbs) and melomels (flavored with fruit) as well as traditional meads. Mead was probably made long before even beer was brewed and can be found all over the Old World, reaching far back into "the dark backward and abysm of time," even as far as ancient Egypt and China. In the Norse myths, mead holds a particularly special standing for its role in the making of poetry and the discovery of wisdom.

In the Norse myth of Kvasir the Poet, wicked dwarves kill Kvasir who, in Padraic Colum's charming retelling (one of my favorites from childhood), "had wisdom, and he had such beautiful words with it, that what he said was loved and remembered by all." The Dwarves combine the poet's blood with honey and make mead from it, storing it in three jars. Curiously, they never drink from the mead; they only want to make sure no one else does. Eventually, the mead falls into the hands of the Giants, who likewise hide it but never use it. In time, Odin the Wanderer, after a series of adventures, comes to the cave where he meets its guardian, the giantess Gunnlöd.

---

2   Euripides, *Bacchae*, trans. Paul Woodruff (Indianapolis, IN: Hackett Publishing Company, 1999), lines 703–11.

The enchantment she is under has turned her into a monster, hideous and decrepit, and she implores Odin, "save me from all this ugliness." The Wanderer takes Gunnlöd's hands, kisses her on the mouth, and "all the marks of ill favor fell from her."[3]

There certainly is something mythic, even mystical, in regard to honey. A natural antiseptic and preservative, it has even been found in the pyramids, still fresh and palatable after thousands of years. No wonder it has for so long been associated with divinity and the indestructible life that so attracted Kerényi.

Honey's metaphysic as image of *poesis* and thereby of creation and wisdom seems to me in need of deeper investigation. What, in a human sense, is creation? What is it we do when we create? In so-called primitive societies, and through the classical era, poetic creation — and thereby artistic creation generally — was associated with prophecy, a kind of divine madness in which the creator's self was instrumental to the divinity speaking through him or her. The poet merely functioned as a conduit, a pipe, for the god in question. Inspiration — literally a *breathing in* of the god — in this understanding is essentially an involuntary act, which is why Plato had reservations about the place of poets in society. The intoxicating effects of mead — almost too obviously — serve as an analogy for the kind of possession that happens during artistic creation; but that isn't the whole story. No doubt, this has something to do with the impossibility of adequately explaining artistic inspiration, a feat no one has yet been able to achieve.

Because human creativity (ubiquitous as it is) defies explanation, recourse to religious language offers what may be the only rhetorical ecosystem up to the task. This is most obvious with the fine arts, of course, but the innovative dimensions of the practical arts likewise trespass into the numinous precincts of the hallows. It is worth noting, then, that the language we use for the creative individual often mimics our language for

3   Padraic Colum, *The Children of Odin* (New York: Macmillan, 1920), 93–101.

divinity: "maker" and "creator." The classical understanding of the poet as both *poeta* (maker, i.e., "craftsman") and *vates* (prophet or seer) is emblematic of the challenge in discernment when the question of creativity arises, providing what Slavoj Žižek calls a "parallax view." Without a doubt, there are elements of training and natural ability involved. For example, I'm a decent musician and poet and know what creativity is in those domains, but while I can handle the tools of the carpenter reasonably well, my skills in that realm are far from anything resembling creativity. And it should be obvious that many "professional poets," for example, are essentially craftsmen or wordsmiths whose work never intrudes into the *templum*, whereas carpenters, glaziers, and stonemasons (think of the great churches of the Middles Ages and Renaissance) can at times not only enter the temple, but make it present to the senses. Creation is nothing if not incarnational.

It is interesting, however, that after the classical era, at least in the West, precious little was said about the role of human creativity until the rise of Romanticism in the late-eighteenth century and through the first half of the nineteenth, though currents of it have persisted, often underground or in the shadows.

The reason for this silence about the role of the maker in the post-classical West is not hard to figure out. Nikolai Berdyaev gets directly to the problem: "There is not one word in the Gospel about creativeness."[4] And not only is the Gospel silent regarding human creation: "We have precepts from the Holy Fathers on fasting and prayer. But we have not, and there could not be, precepts of the Fathers about creativity." This didn't keep Christians from creating, of course, as the marvels of the Middle Ages and the Renaissance attest, but at the very least no one was that concerned with understanding the metaphysics of human creation. One exception may be Paracelsus, that eternal outlier, who claimed, "All natural arts and human

---

4 Nicolas Berdyaev, *The Meaning of the Creative Act*, trans. Donald A. Lowrie (New York: Collier Books, 1962), 91.

wisdom are given by the stars, we are pupils of the stars, and they our teacher. God has ordered everything in the light of Nature that we may learn from it."[5]

With the arrival of the Protestant Reformation, however, a palpable anxiety about human creativity and the allure of the beautiful crept into the Christian psyche which resulted, among other things, in virulent attacks on the Mass as nothing but a performance piece, a falsely pious form of theater. This anxiety reached also to a suspicion of the beauties of the Creation in general, let alone the stars that so inspired Paracelsus. As Eamon Duffy astutely observes, "Iconoclasm was the central sacrament of the reform."[6] This anxiety, habitually erupting into psychosis, pervades the early modern period and is found to a marked degree in even some of the finest poets of the age, particularly Edmund Spenser, John Milton, and even George Herbert. More recently, it haunts the philosophy of Jacques Ellul, which renders his thought, for all his cogent insights into the problems of modernity, austere and off-putting. Reform achieved its *telos* in the Enlightenment, and then it was left to the Romantics to reimagine the role of the maker in human societies.

The Romantics rejected the sterile self-assurance of the modern subject and upheld a vision of being human that both looked back to an integral imagination of medieval Christendom (as in Novalis's *Christianity, or Europe?*) and forward to a transfigured human society. Much of this, as in Wordsworth and, above all, Goethe, had to do with finding a new way of seeing the world. For Wordsworth, the goal was to reenter the garden from which we were expelled and become like children again, as he writes in "Ode: Intimations of Immortality from Recollections of Early Childhood," its language resonant with the theological aesthetic of Thomas Traherne:

---

5   Paracelsus, *Astronomia Magna* in *Paracelsus: Essential Readings*, selected and trans. Nicholas Goodrick-Clarke (Wellingborough, UK: Crucible, 1990), 110.
6   Eamon Duffy, *The Stripping of the Altars: Traditional Religion in England 1400–1580* (New Haven, CT: Yale University Press, 1992), 480.

There was a time when meadow, grove, and stream,
The earth, and every common sight,
To me did seem
Apparelled in celestial light,
The glory and the freshness of a dream.[7]

For Goethe, this project even sought to reform the "gloomy empirical-mechanical-dogmatic torture chamber" that science had become in the wake of Bacon, Descartes, and Newton.[8] For the passionate and radical Percy Bysshe Shelley, like Goethe, the poetic is not restricted to the crafting of verse so much as to the whole of making as implied in the Greek term *poesis*, the activity by which a person brings something into being that did not exist before. This kind of making, then, is potential in every domain of human experience, from the fine and practical arts to philosophy, from economics to politics, and to domestic life. As Shelley writes in The Defence of Poetry, "Poetry is indeed something divine. It is at once the centre and circumference of knowledge; it is that which comprehends all science, the root and blossom of all other systems of thought."[9] But as Keats reminds us, the action of this making influences not only external productions, but is essential to his understanding of Creation as "The vale of Soul-making" and the development of the Self.[10]

The Romantic sensibility, though it fell from favor, never really vanished but persisted in subterranean streams as a companionate "alternative modernity." Often, it intersected with occultism and various forms of mysticism, both orthodox (as in the case of Paul Claudel) as well as heterodox (as in William

---

7   Lines 1–5.
8   Maxim 430, from Johann Wolfgang von Goethe, Maxims and Reflections, trans. Elizabeth Stopp, ed. Peter Hutchinson (London: Penguin Books, 1998), 55.
9   Percy Bysshe Shelley, The Defence of Poetry in Shelley's Poetry and Prose, ed. Donald H. Reiman and Neil Fraistat, Norton Critical Editions (New York: W. W. Norton & Company, 202), 531.
10   John Keats, "Letter to George and Georgiana Keats, 14 February . . . 3 May, 1819" in John Keats, Selected Letters, ed. Robert Giddings, rev. Jon Mee (Oxford: Oxford University Press, 2002), 232.

Butler Yeats). Romanticism is intuitively (if not institution-
ally) religious, concerned with what is sacred, with the Good,
the True, and the Beautiful, so it is no surprise that a movement or aesthetic so concerned with transcendence should
find comrades-at-arms in other movements exiled from the
power structures of the Master Culture. My claim is that the
souls who have felt such a profound attraction to the Occult
Revival of the nineteenth century, to Blavatskian Theosophy
and Anthroposophy, to Guenonian metaphysics, to the New
Age, neo-paganism, and other such movements are driven by
a desire for the sacred they find unavailable in mainstream
forums of religious expression, which are all too often compromised by worldly concerns and politics, if not stomach-turning
scandal. Who wouldn't take a chance on Romanticism when
the institutional is so compromised? It is not for nothing that
Owen Barfield named his book on the contributions of Rudolf
Steiner *Romanticism Comes of Age*.

The idea of this kind of *making* has been all but forgotten in
the age of prefabrication and mechanical reproduction, a point
made long ago by Walter Benjamin. In the fine arts, for example, performances are so often duplicated, whether by analog
or digital methods, that their splendor becomes dissipated in
modernity's ocean of white noise. We treat them as wallpaper. But even wallpaper, William Morris would have argued,
should not be treated as wallpaper. For Morris, the common
things of our homes were not meant to be common things
and the mechanization and banality of even our environments
he viewed as a "desecration" that led ultimately exploitation
and war.[11] He lived in an awareness that "the adventure of
freedom is also always a realisation of beauty and a communion with the earth."[12] Who hasn't recognized the charm, the
individuality, of even a dilapidated barn, exuding a presence

---

11   Jack Lindsay, *William Morris: His Life and Work* (New York: Taplinger
Publishing Company, 1979), 217.
12   Ibid., 378.

that far surpasses that of even the most opulent prefabricated McMansion? What have we lost in the migration from wood, plaster, stone, and brick to Styrofoam, drywall, PVC pipe, and vinyl siding? I remember as a boy going to visit friends in the newly minted subdivisions outside of my hometown of Detroit. All the houses looked alike. It was easy to get lost: a fitting metaphor for our environments and, indeed, for our times.

The malaise that imbues the atmosphere of the subdivision permeates every Walmart, every big box store, every industry, every city council, every political party, burdened as all of them are with the soul-deadening oppression of uninterrogated convention. The egregore, the spirit of the group mind, is without a doubt the spirit of the age.

The egregore, indeed, is that silent participant in each discourse of ours with what Rilke calls "our interpreted world" in the social milieu of the technocratic commons. It is only when we wrestle meaning from the world — the paradigmatic poetic act — that we uncover an altogether different silent interlocutor, the presence of which announces itself by the reprieve of insight. Indeed, there is always a silent participant in our participation with the Things of This World, but the nature of that participant is dependent upon the presence (or lack of presence) we bring to phenomena. Even in their physicality, phenomena always hide something from us. The Cubists tried to solve this problem in art, but a spiritual correlative is likewise undisclosed, though it may all the same come into what Martin Heidegger calls "unconcealment." Is this what we sense in the mysterious being of the dilapidated barn? Similarly, is the emptiness we face in an aisle at Walmart or the cloneworld that is the subdivision not also indicative of the spiritual being of utility?

Art, by which I mean the fruits of the creative act in any domain, is that which frees the human soul from the imprisonment of the utilitarian demiurge: a sophianic deed if ever there were one. As Heidegger writes, "The art work opens up in its own way the Being of beings. This opening up, i.e., the truth of beings, happens in the work. In the art work, the truth of what is has set itself to work. Art is truth setting itself to work."[13] But *quid est veritas?* The true is the holy.

Do we not feel a sense of sacred in the dilapidated barn? We certainly feel it in the forest at times, through works of art, in the *realness* of traditional handcrafts, in the profound magnificence of a Gothic cathedral, in a garden. We don't feel it in a strip mall, in a parking garage, or while encased in drywall and Styrofoam. The holy itself is invisible, yet the structures of the poetic call it forth to presence. Heidegger, contemplating Rilke's *Duino Elegies*, puts it this way:

> In the invisible of the world's inner space, as whose worldly oneness the Angel appears, the haleness of worldly beings becomes visible. Holiness can appear only within the widest orbit of the wholesome. Poets who are of the more venturesome kind are under way on the track of the holy because they experience the unholy as such. Their song over the land hallows. Their singing hails the integrity of the globe of Being.
>
> The unholy, as unholy, traces the sound for us. What is sound beckons to the holy, calling it. The holy binds the divine. The divine draws the god near.[14]

We know this to be true. We have felt the holiness of the barn, of the thatched cottage, of the handmade doorknob, no less than we have of the poem, the sound of a violin in the next room, or a sunset. The question is why we don't seek it more often and tolerate as acceptable alternatives the utilitarian, the mass-produced, and the banal. Everything has a spiritual correlative: it is up to us to decide which it will be.

The Indian sage Sri Aurobindo (1872 – 1950) came to exactly this conclusion about the role of the poetic in human

---

13 Martin Heidegger, *Poetry, Language, Thought,* trans. Albert Hofstadter (New York: Harper & Row, 1971), 39.
14 Ibid., 141.

flourishing. "All art worth the name," he wrote, "must go beyond the visible, must reveal, must show us something that is hidden, and in its total effect not reproduce but create,"[15] words William Blake himself would have been proud to have uttered. Aurobindo, educated at Cambridge, was steeped in the study of the Romantic poets and found much in affinity with their sensibilities, particularly their spiritual courage and rejection of scientific materialism and the clear evidence of what he called "a potent alchemy of transformation" in their work that he attributed to the Celtic wellsprings of the British Isles.[16] Aurobindo anticipated a transfiguration of human societies based on this reality of making, but he knew such isn't guaranteed:

> Greatest of all is the promise of the age that is coming, if the race fulfills its highest and largest opening possibilities and does not founder in a vitalistic bog or remain tied in a materialistic paddock; for it will be an age in which all the worlds are beginning to withdraw their screens from man's gaze and invite his experience, and he will be near the revelation of the Spirit of which they are, as we choose, the obscuring veils, the significant forms and symbols of the transparent raiment. It is as yet unclear to which of these consummations destiny is leading us.[17]

Indeed, it often seems as if the world prefers the obscuring veils to the Real; but there is always a counter-impulse, the spirit that informs all true religion and Romanticism, a spark that can never lose its fire.

So how do we get there?

Part of the answer, I think, lies in *reverie*. Reverie, that state of consciousness (is it even appropriate to call it an "awareness"?) that occupies the *metaxu* between thinking and dreaming seems

---

15   Sri Aurobindo, *The Future Poetry*, with "*Quantitative Metre*" (Pondicherry: Sri Aurobindo Trust, 1997), 8.
16   Ibid., 55.
17   Ibid., 40.

to me to be absolutely necessary to the creative act. And there are many creative acts, living not the least of them. "Poetic reverie gives us the world of worlds," writes Gaston Bachelard. "Poetic reverie is a cosmic reverie. It is an opening to a beautiful world, to beautiful worlds. It gives to the I a non-I which belongs to the I: my non-I."[18] The outlines between subject and object become diaphanous.

Shelley locates reverie, as does Bachelard, in the being of the child, which many of us carry through life: "There are some persons who in this respect are always children. Those who are subject to the state called reverie feel as if their nature were dissolved into the surrounding universe, or as if the surrounding universe were absorbed into their being."[19] Unless you become as a little child, you will never enter the Kingdom of Heaven, for "Creation is but self-forgetful play."[20] Nor will the Kingdom of Heaven enter you. If play is the work of the child, as Piaget observed, then those who remember how to play must be those who most easily pass into reverie, a capacity not limited by age.

Reverie leads to a kind of contemplation, not in a formal, procedural sense, but in the way of facilitating an openness to the world that is, unfortunately, bred out of us by a deadening educational system and the arid expanses of politics and economics as they are typically conceived and practiced. Contemplation, I say, is primarily our natural state of being as it renders us mindful of both God and Creation, as well as their *metaxu*, Sophia. Contemplation, in its way, may be more disciplined than reverie, but it is likewise one of the natural gifts with which we are endowed — as natural as the five senses; as natural as the capacity to love. Acts taken from reverie and

18   Gaston Bachelard, *The Poetics of Reverie: Childhood, Language, and the Cosmos*, trans. Daniel Russell (Boston: Beacon Press, 1969), 13.
19   Percy Bysshe Shelley, *On Life*, in *Shelley's Poetry and Prose*, 507.
20   *Talking with Angels*, transcribed by Gitta Mallasz, translated by Robert Hinshaw, assisted by Gitta Mallasz and Lela Fischili, revised (Daimon Verlag, 1992), 185.

contemplation are not fashioned or performed for their own sake. Rather, these creative acts become acts of wholesomeness and, at times, acts of the holy.

This is not to say that the creative act should be naive, or prudish and self-conscious, the latter two of which attitudes drove Spenser and Milton to the point of neurosis. Michelangelo's nudes, for example, have been charged with flirting with the pornographic, but that certainly says more about audience reception than it does about creative inspiration. The Protestant Reformation with its intrinsic iconoclasm fairly reeked with anxieties about artistic representation, but Michelangelo's Catholic contemporaries (and our own) were by no means immune to the aesthetics of shame. For instance, when the papal Master of Ceremonies, Biagio da Cesena, was offended by the nudes the great artist was painting in his Last Judgment, he scurried off to tattle to the Pope. In repayment, Michelangelo painted Cesena as a figure in hell, entwined by a serpent and crowned with horns. When Cesena complained to the Holy Father, he was informed that it was too bad Michelangelo hadn't painted him in Purgatory: because even the pope can't get someone out of hell. Immodest modesty never knows how to recognize the beautiful as it shines through eros. Indeed, are Michelangelo's nudes not a meditation upon the prelapsarian body, before the arrival of shame and before God asked Adam, "Who told you you were naked?"

The beauty of the Renaissance was that it allowed a vision of being human full of hope, illuminated by divinity. This despite the ravages of plague, war, conflict, and the usual tragedies attendant upon our condition. The Reformation destroyed all (or almost all) of that, and pessimism, materialism, and utilitarianism followed in its wake. The universe was at last disenchanted. What is this quintessence of dust? Ravaged by disenchantment, our world cries out for redemption, even though those cries often come by way of cynicism and ridicule. Only a god can save us.

The creative act, then, is ultimately a theurgic act, an act of divine healing that changes the structure of the cosmos. This is not to say that the theurgic act, the creative act in its essence, is in any way identical with the bourgeois "being creative," which is nothing but a cosmetic refinement of the banal. The theurgic act is salvific, redemptive. As Berdyaev says, "The theurge, working together with God, creates the cosmos; creates beauty as being."[21]

Perhaps there is no more fitting image of theurgy than that of the bees and the making of honey. Of all the facets of my farm, the apiary is by far the most mysterious, from the making of honey to be sure, but no less in the sacrificial drama of the swarm, when the old queen gives up her home to the virgin queen and leaves with her retinue to find a new dwelling. As Virgil writes, "some have taught that the bees have received a share of the divine intelligence, and a draught of heavenly ether, for God, they say, pervades all things, earth and sea's expanse and heaven's depth; from Him the flocks and herds and beasts of every sort draw, each at birth, the slender stream of life."[22]

Virgil also tells of a practice not many modern beekeepers would venture: the raising of bees in the rotting carcass of a bullock. After a suitable location is found, Virgil writes,

> Then a bullock is sought, one just arching his horns on a brow of two summers' growth. Spite of all his struggles, both his nostrils are stopped up, and the breath of his mouth; then he is beaten to death, and his flesh is pounded to a pulp through the unbroken hide. As thus he lies, they leave him in his prison, and strew beneath his sides broken boughs, thyme, and fresh cassia. This is done when the zephyrs begin to stir the waves, ere the meadows blush with their fresh hues, ere the chattering

21   Nicolas Berdyaev, *The Meaning of the Creative Act*, 230.
22   Virgil, *Georgics* 4.219–24. In Virgil, *Eclogues, Georgics, Aeneid* I–VI, trans. H. Rushton Fairclough, rev. ed. (Cambridge, MA: Harvard University Press, 1956).

swallow hangs her nest from the rafters. Meantime the moisture, warming in the softened bones, ferments, and creatures of wondrous wise to view, footless at first, soon with buzzing wings as well, swarm together, and more and more essay the light air, until, like a shower pouring forth from summer clouds, they burst forth, or like arrows from the string's rebound, when the light-armed Parthians enter on the opening battle.

What god, ye Muses, forged for us this device?[23]

Like the uncanny rites of the Maenads, the violent and even gruesome spectacle of the sacrifice of the bullock points to a life (zoē) that even death cannot destroy, a life that is the source of the creative-theurgic act. Indeed, have those who have been brought to death's threshold and returned not also spoken of marvels beyond the veil? Death is not the worst thing that can happen.

The truly creative act, in whichever domain, accesses and partakes of this divine life, full of mystery and wonder. This is theurgy, the life to which we are called. Anything else is merely a simulacrum of life and belongs to the realm of the dead.

---

23   Ibid., 4.299–315.

5
Eleanor Farjeon and the Singing God

I DIDN'T KNOW IT UNTIL VERY LATE, BUT two of my all-time favorite songs boast lyrics written by the British poet, playwright, librettist, and maker of (ostensibly) children's stories, Eleanor Farjeon (1881–1965).

I've known the first song since childhood courtesy of Cat Stevens's (aka Yusuf Islam) glorious recording "Morning Has Broken," the lyrics of which had previously been adapted for the Anglican hymnal, though Farjeon's original title was "A Morning Song (for the First Day of Spring)." The words, so simple and unencumbered by pretense, capture with immediacy the splendor of Eden that perpetually shines through the created world, though usually passes by our weakened powers of perception:

> Morning has broken,
> Like the first morning,
> Blackbird has spoken
> Like the first bird;
> Praise for the singing,
> Praise for the morning,
> Praise for them springing
> Fresh from the Word.
>
> Sweet the rain's new fall,
> Sunlit from heaven,
> Like the first dewfall
> On the first grass;
> Praise for the sweetness,
> Of the wet garden,

Sprung in completeness
Where His feet pass.

Mine is the sunlight,
Mine is the morning,
Born of the one light
Eden saw play;
Praise with elation,
Praise every morning,
God's re-creation
Of the new day.

The other piece enshrining her lyrics is one that's haunted me since my days as a Waldorf teacher, the subtly sublime Christmas hymn "People, Look East!" that likewise attends to nature's simultaneous participation in and revelation of the Glory of the Lord.

Farjeon wrote the lyrics for a number of other hymns, as well as a children's book, *Ten Saints*. Surprisingly, she wrote all of them long before she ever formally became a Christian. Indeed, it was not until 1951 that Farjeon was baptized, "a very old baby of 70" in her own words, and received into the Catholic Church. [1] She became an ardent Catholic, though rather a bohemian one, whose attitude toward Confession and the weekly obligation to attend Mass were colored by the spirit of improvisation. In this she was not unlike the great sophiologist, Vladimir Solovyov who maintained a cosmic understanding of "the Church," while in no way being oblivious to the more political concerns of Christianity at the ground level.

Unfortunately, Farjeon is more or less excluded from serious scholarly consideration as a "children's author." My recent excavation of the scholarship on Farjeon, in fact, came up nearly completely empty, a fate I suspect has more to do with her gender than her genius: you don't see Tolkien or Lewis dismissed like that. And Farjeon's Christian imagination is in

---

1   Denys Blakelock, *Eleanor: Portrait of a Farjeon* (London: Victor Gollancz, Ltd., 1966), 59.

every way equal to theirs, if not superior.

Her relative neglect is tragic indeed, for Eleanor Farjeon's vision offers an antidote to the soporific that is the technocratic age. Farjeon's poetic vision is nothing if not sophiological. Like the English Romantics, nature speaks to Farjeon, and through it she hears the voice of divinity as she so eloquently puts sit in her poem "The World's Amazing Beauty," originally found in her 1918 collection, *Sonnets and Poems*. The poem is nearly a précis for sophiological insight:

> The world's amazing beauty would make us cry
> Aloud; but something in it strikes us dumb.
> Beech-forests drenched in sunny floods
> Where shaking rays and shadows hum,
> The unrepeated aspects of the sky,
> Clouds in their lightest and their wildest moods,
> Bare shapes of hills, June grass in flower,
> The sea in every hour,
> Slopes that one January morning flow
> Unbrokenly with snow,
> Peaks piercing heaven with motions sharp and harsh,
> Slow-moving flats, grey reed and silver marsh,
> A flock of swans in flight
> Or solitary heron flapping home,
> Orchards of pear and cherry turning white,
> Low apple-trees with rosy-budded boughs,
> Streams where young willows drink and cows,
> Earth's rich ploughed loam
> Thinking darkly forward to her sheaves,
> Water in Autumn spotted with yellow leaves,
> Light running overland,
> Gulls standing still above their images
> On strips of shining sand
> While evening in a haze of green
> Half-hides
> The calm receding tides —
> What in the beauty we have seen in these
> Keeps us still silent? something we have not seen?

As often happens in souls attuned to Sophia, there is what we could call a pagan streak in Farjeon, which is perhaps most obvious in the title of her first collection (and its first poem), *Pan-Worship* (1908). As she writes there,

> O virgin Greece, standing with naked feet
> In the morning dews of the world against the light
> Of an infant dawn! old Greece, ever-young Greece,
>
> The pagan in my blood, the instinct in me
> That yearns back, back to nature-worship, cries
> Aloud to thee! [2]

Farjeon knew that to be a good Christian, one need not destroy the groves sacred to Apollo or Pan. Such zeal, for her, had no place in the religion of Christ:

> I cannot unite with those who serve destruction so idol-atrously. Too often their zeal confuses the false worshipper therein, and seeks to reduce both to common ruin. Theirs is the intolerant Christian spirit that shattered the world's wonder at Ephesus in the fourth century of Christ — Christ's self already forgotten. . . . Old legends where beauty walks in mystic light are true legends still, and ancient altars where faith once lit its starry flame are holy places still, for they have been breathed on by eternal types. [3]

Not everything was glory for Farjeon, however, though, at least in her poetry, even those aspects of life characterized by regret or suffering are capable of revelation. In her sonnet, "Farewell, you children that I might have borne," Farjeon, who never married or had children (though she did fall in love and have a thirty year cohabiting relationship with a man), meditates on such a condition:

---

2 Eleanor Farjeon, *Pan-Worship and Other Poems* (London: Elkin, Mathews, 1908), 10.
3 Eleanor Farjeon, *Trees* (London, 1914), 14–15.

> Farewell, you children that I might have borne.
> Now must I put you from me year by year,
> Now year by year the root of life be torn
> Out of this womb to which you were so dear,
> Now year by year the milky springs be dried
> Within the sealed-up fountains of my breast,
> Now year by year be to my arms denied
> The burden they would break with and be blessed. [4]

It is as a sophianic poet that Farjeon's power — and delightful strangeness — lies, as in the poem "Double Beauty" with its echoes of Henry Vaughan's "Cock-Crowing" and its clear sophiological understanding of the world:

> Love of the light compels that lark to singleness
> And brims his tiny body with a spark;
> The nightingale draws music from a spring
> Out of the bosom of the belovèd dark;
> But on man's twofold nature God has breathed
> The double soul of beauty like a spell,
> And dark in light or light in darkness sheathed
> His spirit still must sing the miracle. [5]

And so may we always sing. *Singing*, in fact, is the key to understanding Farjeon's work, in which everything sings: people, trees, animals, and, especially, divinity. This is the centerpiece of her sophiology and the manner by which she calls Sophia out of exile.

I doubt that Eleanor Farjeon (called "Nellie" by family and friends — and the temptation is great for me to do the same!) had ever heard the word "Sophiology." Nevertheless, the sophianic shines through her work with a delightful and unabashed boldness. Instead of the word "Sophia," Farjeon's preferred image for the glory of God shining through Nature is Pan, the god of the woods and fields. As Eugene McCarraher explains, "Once upon a time the world was enchanted.

---

4 In *Sonnets and Poems*.
5 From *Dream-Songs for the Belovèd* (London, 1911).

Rocks, trees, rivers, and rain pulsated with invisible forces, powers that enlivened and determined the affairs of tribes and empires as well. Though beholden to the caprice or providential design of a variety of spirits and deities, the world of enchantment could be commanded by magic or humbly beseeched through prayer."[6] This "once upon a time" did not exist for Nellie Farjeon. The invisible forces of Nature, deriving ultimately from God, were real to her, and poetry was her method of prayer.

Many allegedly Christian readers often exhibit a kind of revulsion to the name of Pan — a goat-footed god with horns many associate with the Devil. But the Evil One is never described in such terms in scripture; in fact, he actually sounds more like a politician. In medieval iconography, the Evil One is typically shown as a monster or dragon, but never in any way similar to the god of the woods and fields.

Looking to antiquity, we can find at least two responses to a story Plutarch shares regarding Pan in De defectu oraculorum.[7] According to the Greek historian, a sailor named Thamus heard a voice, apparently at the time of the crucifixion of Christ, which spoke to him: "Thamus, are you there? When you reach Palodes, take care to proclaim that the great god Pan is dead." The early Christian historian Eusebius interpreted this utterance as proof that the ancient gods (Pan the one most venerated by the agrarian peasantry), were no more as a result of Christ's death and resurrection.[8] There is another tradition, however, that suggests the voice was actually speaking of Christ and was horrified at the death of the God of Nature, that the God of Zoë could die. Farjeon was drawing on the second tradition in which Christ, the Lord of the Dance, is He Who Lives.

---

6   Eugene McCarraher, The Enchantments of Mammon: How Capitalism Became the Religion of Modernity (Cambridge, MA: Harvard University Press, 2019), 1.
7   Moralia, 5.17.
8   Eusebius, Praeparatio Evangelica, 5.

Her invocation of Pan as cipher for Christ in "Pan-Worship" is simultaneously a lament for the disappearance of the sacred from human life and civilization, which she saw as inseparable from the modern disenchantment of Nature. The tone of the poem is melancholic, not one of Farjeon's usual registers, yet not without hope: "O Pan, old Pan, / Shall I not see thee stirring in the stone, / Crack thy confinement, leap forth — *be again?*"[9] She's not speaking of any antique deity save the one domesticated by theology, restricted by centuries of habit, and exiled by modernity: and that deity yet lives. Farjeon takes it upon herself to revive his proper worship:

> God of Nature,
> Thrice hailing thee by name with boisterous lungs
> I will thrill thee back from the dead ages, thus:
> *Pan! Pan! O Pan! bring back thy reign again*
> *Upon the earth!*...
> Numb pointed ears, ye hear
> Only the wash and whisper of far waters,
> The pale green waters of thin distant Springs
> Under the pale green light of distant moons
> Washing upon the shores of the old, old world
> With a foam of flowers, a foam of whispering flowers.[10]

Just replace the name "Pan" with "Christ." Chilling and, sadly, accurate.

In her delightful little book *Trees*, Farjeon acts the role of fabulist that further illuminates her point in a more joyous cadence than in "Pan-Worship." Her story is one of an encounter with Chronos, god of time, with "the Hoofed One." Chronos is deadly serious, rational. Not so his interlocutor:

> "Have you then found a bigger star than mine?" cried the Old One in alarm. "With many moons and brighter hoops of fire? What were you doing while we were raking the firmament?"

---

9   *Pan-Worship*, 11. Nellie's emphasis.
10   Ibid., 11–12. Her emphasis.

"Dancing, Old Bones, dancing."

"And where?"

"On earth, with man my brother."[11]

Chronos is scandalized that the Hoofed One doesn't hold himself more aloof from those who should worship him. He warns that man will despise him. "O Chronos!" exclaims the Friend of Man, "how he will love me. Though he forget my name, and names no star for me, how he will love me."[12] Farjeon's God is the God children know, the One who speaks to them through the Creation. As she writes, "For since the divine Pagan dares to exist in harmony with the eternal spirit, trees, which are the temples of Pan, are also prophets of God. He laid his secret within all his creations as they passed through his hands."[13] Farjeon's god is a dancing god.

Christ is not only a dancing god in Farjeon's eyes. In the apocryphal *Acts of John*, the Lord leads the apostles in a dance on Holy Thursday, a ritual of great beauty and wonder. There Jesus tells them, "'Before I am delivered up to them, let us sing a hymn to the Father, and go forth to what lieth before us.' So he commanded us to make as it were a ring, holding one another's hands, and himself standing in the middle."[14] He then begins to sing and lead them in a dance. "Grace is dancing. I would pipe, dance all of you! Amen. I would mourn, lament all of you! Amen."[15] Jesus reveals to them that the dance is itself the Cross, the axis of the world; and he tells them that this is a mystery. Long after the composition of *The Acts of John*, Jesus was memorialized in similar terms by folk tradition in the hymn "Tomorrow Shall Be My Dancing Day," which begins,

---

11   *Trees*, 10.

12   Ibid.

13   Ibid., 20.

14   Bernhard Pick (trans. and ed.), *The Apocryphal Acts of Paul, Peter, John, Andrew, and Thomas* (Chicago: The Open Court Publishing Co., 1909), 94.

15   Ibid., 95.

> Tomorrow shall be my dancing day;
> I would my true love did so chance
> To see the legend of my play,
> To call my true love to my dance.

And which, after recapitulating the life, death, and resurrection, sings:

> Then up to heaven I did ascend,
> Where now I dwell in sure substance
> On the right hand of God, that man
> May come unto the general dance.

This all resurfaced again in the early 1960s with the modern hymn, "The Lord of the Dance" written by Sydney Carter. Nellie Farjeon would approve, for it was she who wrote: "And the beast who stands midway betwixt man and God has danced ever since, and men have worshipped beneath his temples, and the few have known it and the many have known it not."[16]

It might be easy to overlook the intimacy with the divinity Farjeon addresses through the image of Pan, seeing that Pan's intimacy is a universal one and the posterity of mankind itself. But there is another intimacy, a very personal one, that illumines her poetry with the language of bridal mysticism.

Bridal mysticism (*Brautmystik*), as we have seen, is a mystical language found in the writings of the medieval period, particularly with the Beguine communities of Belgium, The Netherlands, and parts of France. Grounded in the erotic longing of the Song of Songs, the writings of the Beguines speak of union with God through abandonment and the intoxication of love. Mechthild of Magdeburg's God speaks precisely this language:

> Your mountains shall dissolve in love;
> Your enemies shall gain no part of you;
> Your field has been penetrated by the warm sun;
> Your fruit has nevertheless remained unspoiled;

---

16 *Trees*, 13.

And in my kingdom you shall be a new bride;
And there I shall give you a delicious kiss on the mouth,
That my entire Godhead shall soar through your soul. [17]

Farjeon, in her own inimitable way, made this erotic language her own.

In "Dream Songs for the Belovèd," Farjeon adopts such an erotic language and, as in Sufi poetry, the distinctions between the earthly beloved and God dissolve. In the second of the Dream Songs, she makes this quite explicit:

So from the silence of the darkest hour
The light that is a miracle in my soul
Distils the presence of the Well-Belov'd
    And I possess the image in him of God. [18]

In the first of the Dream Songs, she ends with a proclamation of the divine mystery of eros:

But I have found a still land of neither pain nor passion,
No loss because no giving there, no gain since no desire,
And the great silent light of the Belovèd's spirit brooding
With the soul of all time there, made empty of desire. [19]

This divine mystery is the great antinomy wherein eros is the vehicle of annihilation, which was the central insight of the Beguine martyr Marguerite Porete, an insight that even her burning at the stake as a heretic could not extinguish.

In her sonnet "Thy glance is lovelier than the glance of the moon," Farjeon reiterates the power of divine love to obliterate all sense, even the sense of self, in union with the Belovèd:

The stones I tread no longer solid are,
These narrow houses all are built of air,
Nay, are they on this star, or on that star

---

17   Mechthild of Magdeburg, *The Flowing Light of the Godhead*, trans. Frank Tobin (New York: Paulist Press, 1998), 149.
18   *Dream Songs of the Belovèd*, 9.
19   Ibid., 8.

Distantly trembling? Am I here or there?
Love, love, I know not what is near and far,
I am with thee and thou art everywhere.[20]

This sense of disorientation so familiar to lovers mirrors beautifully the correlate disorientation of one lost in Divine Love. In the third Dream Song, she further explores this dynamic:

I seem to walk as a shadow in Love's shadow,
I seem to have always known what love might be
And beyond knowledge passed to the great tranquility.[21]

Then she moves to the image of "the smoking rose-torch," which evokes the *spina alba* of ancient Roman marriage processions. But Farjeon has a different consummation in mind:

I seem to have gained light without the longing,
For lo! even as the smoking rose-torch came
Within my hands, red flame turned smokeless silver flame.

Now in my dreams I tread an asphodel meadow
Where move the lovers out of the dreamful past.
"Dead lovers, how is it with you?"

                              "It is well at last,
Sister," reply their eyes about me thronging,
And all the phantoms of that immortal flight
Carry their torches still, and all the flames are white.[22]

In classical mythology, the Asphodel Meadows are the realm of the dead. In the poem, then, desire is the vehicle for the purification of desire, and heaven is a wedding.

In the poem "In Love's House," Nellie Farjeon makes her most explicit statement of the bridal mysticism that inhabits her work, a poem that opens with the line, "Love the God has at last unclouded his eyes." Farjeon ventriloquizes through God the speaker of the poem that she may set bad theology aright:

---

20 *Sonnets and Poems*, 13.
21 *Dream Songs for the Belovèd*, 10.
22 Ibid.

"I it is colour my chosen ones, never they me,
I am not theirs to possess, they are mine, they are mine.
Did you believe I was given to you as a gift,
Something to treasure and care for and handle and clothe?
Lo! it is you are my gift to be treasured and clothed,
Fashion no garments for me, mine has fallen on you.

"How should men colour me? sing me? array me in light?
How should they think me, conceive me, endow me with
    form?
Mine is the thought, the conception none other's than mine,
You and the children of men are the birth I bring forth,
Not within you do I enter, you enter me.

"All is expressed for you finally here in my heart.
Struggle no more to express me. My silences sing."[23]

At the age of thirty, and a full forty years before her formal entrance into the Church, Farjeon proved a more perspicacious and capable theologian than many who have appeared either before or since. Nellie Farjeon's God sings even in silence.

Music was, in fact, an important element to her life. Her elder brother Harry was an accomplished composer and taught at the Royal Academy of Music, and Eleanor provided the libretto for his opera *Fioretto* which was produced at the Academy in 1899 when Harry was only twenty-one and Eleanor but eighteen. Her friend and confidante Denys Blakelock described her as "steeped in music and a Wagnerite" who, though she loved talking on the telephone, would take the receiver off the hook when she was listening to opera on the radio.[24]

Music, for Nellie Farjeon, was a vehicle for divinity as well as a source of life. Its transformative powers were not lost on her and appear repeatedly in her verse and prose works. In the pastoral "Colin Clout, Come Home Again!" she outlines these miraculous powers:

---

23 Ibid. 14–15.
24 Denys Blakelock, *Eleanor: Portrait of a Farjeon*, 47.

Hark! I hear a shepherd's pipe
With three notes of music wipe
Discord from this troubled star;
I hear tumultuous gladness shake
The marrows of the land awake,
Where old slumbering visions are
. . . .
O piping shepherd-reed at play,
Blown with a poet's golden breath,
How innocent, as full of faith
As children's hearts are, 'gins to beat
In the world's bosom at my feet! [25]

These lines may appear to be something written for children, but that only proves how jaded is an eye that reads them so. Nellie Farjeon never lost the capacity to see with the eyes of a child and, so, stayed forever youthful. As Blakelock describes her, "Eleanor Farjeon was a born Fairy Godmother," who possessed an indefatigable "confidence in life and in the goodness of her fellow human beings." [26] She wanted to "re-teach us how to sing." [27] Her description of the protagonist of the poem "The Singer," is, indeed, an accurate description of the poet:

There while about her golden head
the shadows and the low light played,
She eagerly and softly read
The shining songs her soul had made.
. . . .
Death and life, and life and death,
Divinely in her vision smiled;
She spoke them with the silver breath
Half of angel, half of child. [28]

God, the source of all goodness for Nellie Farjeon, is quite naturally the source of all song; for he is the archetypal singer.

---

25 *Sonnets and Poems*, 24–25.
26 Denys Blakelock, *Eleanor: Portrait of a Farjeon*, 93 and 94.
27 From "Colin Clout, Come Home Again!" in *Sonnets and Poems*, 27.
28 *Sonnets and Poems*, 34.

In "Wild Hyacinth" Farjeon instructs the trembling flower about this divinity:

> And heaven I know is expressed in you because you were
>   loved of a God,
> You are nourished by tears of celestial dew because from
>   his hand flew death,
> And your quivering singing loveliness was born of his
>   quivering breath
>   That sighed its twilight of sorrows into sod:
> For the heart of the lover you wreathed of old was the
>   heart of the Singing God. [29]

Furthermore, the hyacinth shines in the figure of Christ, "the beautiful boy the Great Ones adored and destroyed" and has become the "measureless beauty conceived of the sorrow and love of the Lord of Light!"[30] Nellie Farjeon wants for us to seek "Just higher than the summit of the soul — / Music half-heard, song uncontainable."[31]

Music saturates the cosmos for Nellie Farjeon. I imagine she found the restoration scene from Shakespeare's *Pericles, Prince of Tyre* particularly moving: "The music of the spheres! List, my Marina" which presages the theophany of the goddess Diana. Even more is Caedmon's call — the foundational event of English literature — germane to Nellie Farjeon's poetic spirituality; for Caedmon was given the task by an angel to "Sing me the Creation." Eleanor Farjeon never stopped singing the Creation.

The poet's ability to enter the state of reverie is clearly a condition shared with children, and Nellie Farjeon had this quality in abundance. The French philosopher Gaston Bachelard, as we have mentioned, was acutely attentive to reverie and its relationship to childhood and the poetic imagination. "A potential childhood is within us," he writes. "When we go looking

---

29 *Dream Songs for the Belovèd*, 30.
30 Ibid., 30 and 31.
31 From "Never-Known" in *Dream Songs for the Belovèd*, 32.

for it in our reveries, we relive it even more in its possibilities than in reality."[32] In addition, reverie is an eminently restorative act, one by which "the poet's image gives our memories a halo once again."[33] What is the poetry of Eleanor Farjeon but this? She returns to us the halos of childhood. In *Trees*, she describes this phenomenon with a deep and refreshing grace:

> On a shining day I saw very young birches dance like white children knee-deep in blackened heather; and in the dusk of the day I lay upon a slope above still waters among the elfin brakes, pale freakish fronds, little waves curling from the tides of spring about the ankles of pines steeped in their endless revery. The earth, dry-scented with brown needles, fresh-breathing moss, came up with a pulse against my cheek, or it was the pulse in myself beating down to her. Then all the glimpses on the further side of memory were astir, the unheard voices and unseen shapes of a deathless age stole out, and unsurpassable beauty fleeted through the kingdom of the trees.[34]

In this utterance Eleanor Farjeon phrases the sophianic mystery in the clearest, simplest, and most luminous language. She may never have heard the word "Sophiology," but she didn't need to. She breathed it.

Eleanor Farjeon offers us a chance to see and hear once again how the Things of This World "vanish like light dissolved in greater light / Or music drowned in heavenlier music."[35] She shows us the world made new, the Eden that is always already present where "we will re-learn the magic tongue, / And where the meadow-rings are green / Re-seek Titania and her lord,"[36] a sophianic vision if ever there were one: one which calls Sophia out of exile. This sophianic vision is inseparable from the ability

32 Gaston Bachelard, *The Poetics of Reverie: Childhood, Language, and the Cosmos*, trans. Daniel Russell (Boston: Beacon Press, 1969), 101.

33 Ibid., 115.

34 *Trees*, 50–51.

35 From "Morning-Vision" in *Dream Songs for the Beloved*, 47.

36 From "Colin Clout, Come Home Again!" in *Sonnets and Poems*, 25.

to see the world with the eyes of a child, to behold the Glory of the Lord in all its resplendence as it shines through the Creation. This is a gift which the beautiful soul who was Nellie Farjeon shared with the Anglican priest and Metaphysical poet Thomas Traherne, to whom we now turn.

6

The Eyes of
Thomas Traherne

*The light of the body is the eye: if therefore thine eye be single,
thy whole body shall be full of light.*

~: *Matthew* 6 : 22

I DON'T KNOW WHAT COLOR THOMAS TRA-
herne's eyes were, but I know they were filled with light:
single, whole, bright, shimmering with *claritas*. Indeed,
I don't, and neither does anyone else, know what he looked
like, as posterity has left us no drawn or painted image of the
Anglican poet and divine who died at the age of about thirty-
seven in 1674. The only image we have of him is offered to
us in the luminous quality of his writings. But they are more
than enough to allow us to see him.

Of all the great Metaphysical poets — his peers Donne, Herbert, Crashaw, and Vaughan — Traherne is by far the most
mysterious. Virtually unknown before a sheaf of his poetry
was rescued from the bargain bins at two British booksellers
by amateur book collector and antiquarian William Brooke in
the winter of 1896 – 97, the intervening century uncovered an
astounding number of his writings in a series of what can only
be called literary miracles. Only one of Traherne's writings, the
mildly polemical *Roman Forgeries* (1673), had appeared during his
lifetime, while another, *Christian Ethicks* saw publication in 1675,
soon after his death. In 1699, his *Thanksgivings* were published
anonymously as *A Serious and Pathetical Contemplation* and his
Hexameron and *Meditations and Devotions* appeared in various

states and under various titles through the first decades of the eighteenth century, all of them unattributed. The initial discoveries from the nineteenth century were eventually acquired by scholar Bertram Dobbell who identified Traherne as their author. The manuscripts contained a wealth of poetry and the collection of essays of spiritual counsel known ever since as *Centuries* or *Centuries of Meditations*, a discovery *The Quarterly Review* called "one of the most romantic in the annals of English bibliography."[1] In 1964, James Osborn found Traherne's *Select Meditations* in a Birmingham bookseller's catalogue and paid £65 for it, but only later did he discover its authorship (it was not published until 1997). Providentially rescued quite literally from an ash heap in the mid-1960s, *Commentaries of Heaven* was not identified as Traherne's until 1981. In 1997, two more manuscripts were identified as Traherne's: the long poem "The Ceremonial Law" at the Folger Library in Washington, D. C. and *Seeds of Eternity* hiding in the library at Lambeth Palace, London. There is no reason to assume these prodigies have come to an end. It's as if the writing of Traherne *wanted* to be found, but only waited upon the arrival of the proper moment, an acceptable time.

Central to Traherne's religious aesthetic is Christ's admonishment that to enter the Kingdom, one must become like a little child, which is why Traherne again and again returns to the incarnation of the soul as the image of Edenic felicity. His most anthologized poem, "Wonder," begins in precisely this register:

> How like an Angel came I down!
> How Bright are all Things here!
> When first among his Works I did appear!
> O how their GLORY me did Crown?
> The World resembled his *Eternitie*,
> In which my Soul did Walk;

---

1 Quoted in William T. Brooke, "The Story of the Traherne MSS. by Their Finder" in *The Works of Thomas Traherne, Volume V*: Centuries of Meditations, Select Meditations, *with miscellaneous works from the Osborn manuscript*, ed. Jan Ross (Cambridge: D. S. Brewer, 2013), 471–74, at 471.

> And evry Thing that I did see,
> Did with me talk. [2]

For Traherne, this is where our resting in God resides, though it is forgotten or obscured, not by sin so much as by the poisonous effects of society and, above all, by a poisonous education. As he writes in the *Centuries*,

> The first Light which shined in my Infancy in its primitive and innocent clarity was totaly Ecclypsed: insomuch that I was fain to learn all again. If you ask me how it was all Ecclypsed? Truly by the Customs and maners of Men, which like Contrary Winds blew it out: by an innumerable company of other Objects, rude, vulgar, and Worthless Things, that like so many loads of Earth and Dung did over whelm and Bury it: by the Impetuous Torrent of Wrong Desires in all others whom I saw or knew that carried me away and alienated me from it: by a Whole Sea of other Matters and Concernments that Covered and Drowned it: finaly by the Evil Influence of a Bad Education that did not foster and cherish it. [3]

The key for Traherne is to learn how to see again as we did upon our glorious arrival among the Things of This World:

> For Nature teacheth nothing but the truth,
> I'me Sure mine did in my Virgin Youth.
> The very Day my Spirit did inspire,
> The Worlds fair Beauty set my Soul on fire.
> My Senses were Informers to my Heart,
> The Conduits of his Glory Power and Art. [4]

Like Eleanor Farjeon, Traherne uses poetry as the vehicle for

---

2   Unless otherwise indicated, all poetry is taken from Gladys I. Wade (ed.), *The Poetical Works of Thomas Traherne* (New York: Cooper Square Publishers, 1965).

3   *Centuries*, 3.7. All quotations from the *Centuries* are from Anne Ridler (ed.), *Thomas Traherne: Poems, Centuries and Three Thanksgivings* (London: Oxford University Press, 1966).

4   "Nature"

entering once again the pure vision of childhood. The Irish poet A. E. (George William Russell) also identified such a condition as essential to the development of the poet and of poetic reverie: "There may be many other minglings of heaven and earth in childhood which beget a brood which later become desires, thoughts or imaginations, but the earliest are the masters and they lie subtly behind other impulses of the soul."[5] Traherne's intentions may be simple, but they are filled with the troubles and complexities of unlearning all we have learned. As Goethe observed, "Everything is simpler than one can imagine, at the same time more involved than can be comprehended."[6] So it is with the return to felicity.

Perhaps the most intriguing aspect of Traherne's theological aesthetic of becoming a child is the attendant and very palpable egocentricity that accompanies it. Piaget and other child psychologist have, of course, have identified this egocentrism as a preoperational stage that needs to be transcended in order to move into adulthood. Traherne would most certainly agree, but for him the task is to re-enter the Eden of childhood via trust in God and a simultaneous recognition of His sophianic Glory shining through Creation. Traherne's is a redeemed, almost ego-less egocentricity, a purified "I," unbounded, knowing Things as God knows them. In this capacious knowing lives a way of possessing all things by redeeming the fallen acquisitiveness of greed and selfishness. He explains this in "Wonder":

7.
Cursd and Devisd Proprieties.
With Envy, Avarice
And Fraud, those Feinds that Spoyl even Paradice,
Fled from the Splendor of mine Eys.
And so did Hegdes, Ditches, Limits, Bounds,
I dreamd not ought of those,

---

5   A. E., *Song and Its Fountains* (New York: Macmillan, 1932), 1.
6   Maxim 1209 from Johann Wolfgang von Goethe, *Maxims and Reflections*, trans. Elisabeth Stopf; ed. Peter Hutchinson (London: Penguin Books, 1998).

> But wanderd over all mens Grounds,
> And found Repose.

8.

> Proprieties themselvs were mine,
> And Hedges Ornaments;
> Walls, Boxes, Coffers, and their rich Contents
> Did not Divide my Joys, but all combine.
> Clothes, Ribbans, Jewels, Laces, I esteemd
> My Joys by others worn;
> For me they all to wear them seemd
> When I was born.

Traherne's mystical egocentricity is not merely a poetic device for articulating the proper disposition toward God and Creation, he is actually engaged in the *cura animarum*. He was first and foremost a priest, after all, and his writing is pastoral in intent: he wants his reader to look through these poems and into the eye of God.

For Traherne, the vehicle for becoming a child of God is learning how to see, which is why the Eye so fascinates his poetic imagination. As his brother Philip observed, Traherne desired most of all that "he might becom All Ey."[7] Thomas Traherne diagnoses the problem in the *Centuries*, a work he probably wrote explicitly for the English devotional writer Susanna Hopton as epistles of spiritual direction:

> The World is a Mirror of infint Beauty, yet no Man sees it. It is a Temple of Majesty yet no Man regards it. It is a Region of Light and Peace, did not Men Disquiet it. It is the Paradice of God. It is more to Man since he is faln, then it was before. It is the Place of Angels, and the Gate of Heaven. When Jacob waked out of His Dream, he said, *God is here and I wist it not. How Dreadfull is this Place! This is none other, then the Hous of God, and the Gate of Heaven.* [8] (*Centuries* 1.31)

Thus, learning how to see is the first step in becoming as a child, the first step in entering the Kingdom. As Traherne writes in "The Preparative," "'Tis not the Object, but the Light / That maketh Heaven; 'Tis a Purer Sight. / Felicitie / Appears to none but them that purely see."[9] And as he says in "Dumnesse," "It was with Cleerer Eye / To see all Creatures full of Deities." The Creation opens into the Creator, nestled as it is within His heart:

> The visible World is Wonderfully to be Delighted in and
> Highly to be Esteemed, becaus it is the Theatre of GODs
> Righteous Kingdom. . . . here we see His Face in a Glasse,
> and more Dimly behold our Happiness as in a Mirror:
> by faith therfore we are to live, and to sharpen our Ey
> that we may see his Glory. (Centuries 2.97)

Coming to this awareness is a Sophianic Awakening.

Indeed, a sophianic sensibility haunts all of Traherne's writing. In Select Meditations, for example, his language evokes Sophia in Proverbs. "The Lord possessed me in the beginning of his way, before his works of old," says Sophia. "I was set up from everlasting, from the beginning, or ever the earth was" (8:22–23). Traherne: "From all Eternity my Being was with God Almighty."[10] He certainly has the preexistence of the soul in mind here, but his stylistic allusion points to Sophia's simultaneous preexistence at the Creation. And as he reminds his precisian co-religionists who might bristle at such an allegedly Platonic notion, "In Reference to us there is a Past Present and to Come; but in reference to Eternity all is Present."[11]

This awakening for Traherne occurs in a double-movement, a kind of double-intentionality by which the subject's intentionality encounters that of the Deity through their reciprocal attention to Creation. When this happens, phenomena shift, become luminous:

9 Stanza 6.
10 Select Meditations 3.78, from Jan Ross (ed.), The Works of Thomas Traherne, Volume V.
11 Select Meditations 4.28.

His *Wisdom* Shines in Spreading forth the Skie.
His *Power's* Great in Ordering the Sun,
His *Goodness* very Marvellous and High
Appears, in evry Work his Hand hath done.
And all his Works in their varietie,
united or asunder pleas the Eye.[12]

The operative word here is "shines."

When things shine in Traherne's work, we witness the imaginative appearance of Divinity. And by "imaginative" I by no means propose anything artificial, contrived, or hallucinatory. In fact, I mean just the opposite: that these acts encounter the Real, that they trigger a deeper perception for which the five senses only serve as conduits. As William Desmond explains, "Imagination is a *threshold* endowment. It points to an inward otherness, an immanent originality that emerges into freedom from a source it does not initially determine itself."[13] We can say with confidence that Thomas Traherne gives us the methodology for disclosing this immanent originality by which we may behold how the "GODHEAD in his Works doth shine."[14]

Though few poets of Traherne's era, with the notable exception of Henry Vaughan, paid much attention to the Glory of the Lord shining through Creation, a number of mystics and hermetic scientists did (which explains Vaughan's sensibility — he was poet, Hermetic physician, and mystic). In fact mystical images of eyes — the Eyes of God, the Eye of the Heart, the eyes of the seraphim — were nearly standard emblems of the period and adorn an astonishing number of manuscripts and published works. The German mystic Jacob Boehme describes his image of God's eye in *Forty Questions of the Soul*:

---

12 "The Improvement," stanza 3.
13 William Desmond, *Is There a Sabbath for Rest?: Between Religion and Philosophy* (New York: Fordham University Press, 2005), 164.
14 "The Enquirie," stanza 6.

For that is a Globe ☉ like an eye, and is God's Wonder-
Eye, wherein from Eternity all Substances, or things
have been seen or discerned, but *without* substance, as
in a Looking-Glass or Eye; for the Eye is the Eye of the
Abysse of which we have no pen or tongue to write or
speak, only the Spirit of Eternity bringeth the Souls
eye thereinto, and so we see it, else it would remain in
silence mute, and undescribed by his Hand.[15] [See Fig. 1]

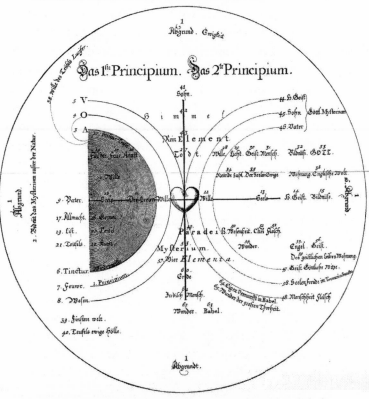

Figure 1: from Jacob Boehme, *Der Weg zu Christo* (1624)

---

15   Question 1.31 from Jacob Behme [Jacob Boehme], *Forty Question of the Soul . . .*, trans. John Sparrow (London, 1665).

The image that accompanies Boehme's description here, clearly diagrammatic and therefore conceptual, abstract, nevertheless serves as an icon of spiritual reality. He really had no sufficient language available to him otherwise. It is no wonder that Dionysius Freher's mysterious and captivating illustrations for Boehme's works repeatedly draw on the image of the eye, so much so that they become paratexts to the writings themselves. The images in these and contemporary Rosicrucian and other Protestant mystical treatises show how Catholic and alchemical iconographic traditions melded and created new visual vocabularies for religious contemplation. [See Fig. 2]

Boehme's works found a wide readership when they were published in John Sparrow and John Elliston's English translations during the mid-seventeenth century, and it is almost impossible to think that Traherne would have been unfamiliar with them. And while I would never dream of suggesting that Traherne was a Behmenist (he was far too independent a thinker to subscribe to any one school of thought, even that of the Anglican Church), he certainly would have found much fruit for spiritual nourishment in the astonishing work of the German mystic.

The English Behmenists and Philadelphians John Pordage and Jane Lead likewise drew on this eye imagery in their mystical speculations.[16] In his treatise *Theologia Mystica*, Pordage provides both a mystical emblem and its explication:

> The round circle represents the Abyssal Globe, the Eye in the midst of the Heart, represents the Father, the Generator of the Son, who is the Heart of the Father: the Heart in the midst of which the Eye is placed, typifies the Son of God, the only begotten of the Father. Co-eternal, Co-essential and Co-equal with him; and the out flowing exit of powers, like a breath, represents the Holy Ghost,

---

16 Pordage cannot technically be called a Philadelphian, since the formal foundation of the Philadelphian Society (which was led by Lead) did not occur until 1696, fifteen years after his death, but he was the founder and guiding spirit of this important, though often neglected, group of Christian universalists.

Figure 2 : from Jacob Boehme, *Theosophische Werke* (Amsterdam, 1682)

proceeding from the Father, through the Heart of the Son. Thus the Birth of the Holy Trinity is manifested, in the opening of the Eye, to be a Trinity in Unity: the Eye is in the Heart, and the Heart is the Eye's Center, and the Spirit is a proceeding Spirit from the Eye and Heart; and thus they are one in another, in one Essence, undivided and inseparable.[17] [See Fig. 3]

Figure 3: from John Pordage, *Theologia Mystica* (London, 1683)

The Eye of God also entered into Jane Lead's seeing, almost, as it were, in technicolor:

In a moment there appeared to me an Azure blue Firmament, so Oriental that nothing of this, in this Visible Orb could parallel with it. Out of the midst hereof was

---

17 John Pordage, *Theologia Mystica, or The Mystic Divinite of the Eternal Invisibles* (London, 1683), 2: 29–30.

a most wonderful Eye, which I saw Sparkling, as with
Flaming Streams from it. Which I am not able to Figure
out, after that manner, in which it did present it self unto
me. . . . There was a Flaming Eye in the midst of a Circle,
and round about it a Rainbow with all variety of Colours,
and beyond the Rainbow in the Firmament, innumerable
Stars all attending this Flaming Eye. From which the Word
said, The Earth and Heavens shall flye, and nothing abide,
but what can live in this Eternal Eye, as ministering Stars
of Glory before the Throne of him: who like this Circling
Eye, which thou hast seen, hath neither Beginning or
End. After this Word it disappeared, leaving its Flaming
Influences upon my Heart.[18] [See Fig. 4]

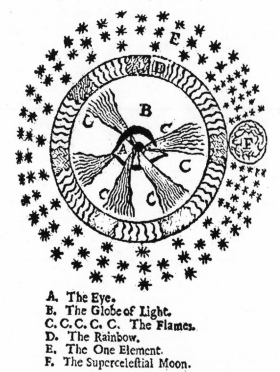

A. The Eye.
B. The Globe of Light.
C. C. C. C. C. The Flames.
D. The Rainbow.
E. The One Element.
F. The Superceleſtial Moon.

Figure 4: from Jane Lead, A Fountain of Gardens, Vol I (London, 1696)

18   Jane Lead, A Fountain of Gardens Watered by the Rivers of Divine Pleasure . . .
[part 1] (London, 1696), 263–64.

The hermetic theologian and Paracelsian physician Robert Fludd also contemplated the mysteries of God's eye in his work. Fludd, more than Pordage and Lead (though the former did have some medical training), was an important scientist of the period and engaged in heated debate with some of the leading scientists of the then-burgeoning Scientific Revolution, Pierre Gassendi and Johannes Kepler not the least of them. He was deeply interested in optics, but not from a purely mechanical or materialist standpoint. First of all, he argued that God's primal creative act was achieved through an act of seeing. According to Fludd's thinking, if the human eye is vessel of light, then the eye of God is that by which God created with the *Fiat lux* and was by definition splendor itself, "the Light of the World."[19] Secondly, he interpreted the eye in terms of the Holy Trinity, with the sclera corresponding to the Father, the cornea to the Son, and the pupil to the Spirit, the Spirit rushing forth at the Creation [see Fig. 5].[20] As Urszula Szulakowska observes, for Fludd, "it was the optical rays of light emanating from God's divine vision which created, sustained, and reabsorbed the universe."[21]

The cultural milieu that was so fascinated by what we can call "the Optics of Mysticism" found its poetic voice in Thomas Traherne. The phenomenology of vision, the act by which what is external to the self enters the self, offered a paradigm of reciprocity that appealed to Traherne because it is true to both Nature and Divinity. "An Object Seen," he writes,

> is in the Faculty Seeing it, and by that in the Soul of the Seer, after the Best of Maners. Wheras there are eight maners of In-being of an Object in a Faculty is the Best of all. Dead Things are in a Room containing them in a vain maner; unless they are Objectively in the Soul of a

19   Robert Fludd, *Utriusque Cosmi Historia* . . . part 1 (Oppenheim, 1617), 164.
20   Robert Fludd, *Utriusque Cosmi Historia* . . . part 2 (Oppenheim, 1619), 26.
21   Urszula Szulakowska, *The Alchemy of Light: Geometry and Optics in Late Renaissance Alchemical Illustration* (Leiden, NL, 2000), 169.

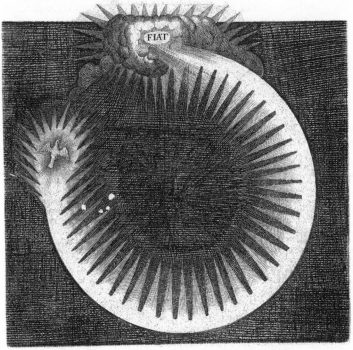

Figure 5: from Robert Fludd, *Utriusque Cosmi
Historia* . . . part 2 (Oppenheim, 1619)

Seer. The Place and the Thing Placed in it, being both in
the Understanding of a Spectator of them. Things Dead
in Dead Place Effect nothing. But in a Living Soul, that
seeth their Excellencies, they Excite a Pleasure answering
to their value, a Wisdom to Embrace them, a Courage
not to Forsake them, a Lov of their Donor, Praises and
Thanksgivings; and a Greatness and a Joy Equal to their
Goodness. And all Ages are present in my Soul, and all
Kingdoms, and GOD Blessed forever. And thus Jesus
Christ is seen in me and dwelleth in me, when I believ
upon Him. And thus all Saints are in me, and I in them.
And thus all Angels and the Eternity and Infinity of GOD
are in me for evermore. I being the Living TEMPLE and
Comprehensor of them. Since therfore all other ways of

> In-being would be utterly vain, were it not for this: And
> the Kingdom of God (as our Savior saith, this Way) is
> within you. (*Centuries* 1.100)

That is, through vision (and, by extension, all the senses) we
enter the Kingdom because the Kingdom thereby enters us.
The organs of sensation, then, are avenues for the entrance of
Divinity into the soul; and Creation itself is a sense organ for
Divinity. As Goethe observed, "If you want to deny that nature
is a divine organ, you might as well deny all revelation."[22]
Thomas Traherne's entire body of work discloses how Nature is,
indeed, a divine organ that, when reverently engaged, reveals
the Maker of All Things. And this spiritual phenomenon only
transpires once we have learned how to see. This is a fundamental sophiological proposition.

Traherne's interest in the "eye-I" homophone is integral to
his disclosure of the mysterious relationship of God and Man,
and it is difficult for the attentive reader of Traherne to miss
this connection, so often does it occur in his work. What is not
recognized, however, is how Traherne extends this homoph-
onological poesis in the direction of affirmation: "Aye." My
claim is that, though the word does not appear in Traherne's
poetry or prose, the affirmative "Aye!," the existential "Yes!"
(that so intrigued James Joyce) watermarks all of the poet's
writing. "What a World would this be," he writes, "were evry
thing Beloved as it ought to be!" (*Centuries* 2.67). It doesn't get
any more affirmative than this. For Traherne, I = eye = aye.

Becoming a child, then, for Traherne is the both the pre-
liminary stage and *telos* of his method. And it is a method, as
he writes in the first of the second Century:

> Wil you see the Infancy of this sublime and celestial
> Greatness? Those Pure and Virgin Apprehensions I had
> from the Womb, and that Divine Light wherewith I was
> born, are the Best unto this Day, wherin I can see the

---

22 *Maxims and Reflections*, No. 810.

Universe. By the Gift of GOD they attended me into the World, and by his Special favor I remember them till now. Verily they seem the Greatest Gifts His Wisdom could bestow, for without them all other Gifts had been Dead and Vain. They are unattainable by Book, and therfore I will teach them by Experience. Pray for them earnestly: for they will make you Angelical, and wholy Celestial. Certainly Adam in Paradice had not more sweet and Curious Apprehension of the World, then I when I was a child.

When he reenters this state of reverie, Traherne, as if a Lazarus rising from the tomb, returns to the Realm of the Living. The language of this awakening shimmers with wonder and the intoxication of the Good:

> The Corn was Orient and Immortal Wheat, which never should be reaped, nor ever was sown. I thought it had stood from Everlasting to Everlasting. The Dust and Stones of the Street were as Precious as GOLD. The Gates were at first the End of the World, The Green Trees when I saw them first through one of the Gates made my Heart to leap, and almost mad with Extasie, they were such strange and Wonderfull Things: The Men! O what Venerable and Reverend Creatures did the Aged seem! Immortal Cherubims! And yong Men Glittering and Sparkling Angels and Maids strange Seraphic Pieces of Life and Beauty! Boys and Girles Tumbling in the Street, and Playing, were moving Jewels. I knew not that they were Born or should Die. But all things abided Eternaly as they were in their Proper Places. Eternity was Manifest in the Light of the Day, and som thing infinit Behind evry thing appeared: which talked with my Expectation and moved my Desire. (*Centuries* 3.3)

But such an illumined state of being could not last in a world of misguided desires and an education disfigured by utility. As Traherne finishes the meditation, "So that with much adoe I was corrupted; and made to learn the Dirty Devices of this

World. Which now I unlearn, and becom as it were a little Child again, that I may enter into the Kingdom of GOD."

Traherne's "becoming a child," then, is clearly not a regression into an infantile state ensconced in the womb and sunken in the oceanic feeling Freud associated with what he thought of as the puerility of religion. As Robert Ellrodt, one the finest critics of Metaphysical poetry has observed, "His childhood is not a distant glory but 'a Sphere' in which the visions of the child and the thoughts of the man are enclosed."[23] That is, Traherne offers us the incredibly simple, but eminently difficult, proposition that we might, too, become as children and enter the Kingdom as the Kingdom simultaneously enters into us.

Finally, what we find in Traherne, or, rather, the gift he gives us, is the sense of abiding grace that permeates every syllable of his *oeuvre*. He becomes the Christian psychopomp, the guide of souls, in a most literal sense: for the activity of reading, and above all of the *lectio divina*, of his poetry inhabits the demesne of the *cura animarum*. He doesn't browbeat us, like John Wesley, with our wretchedness and the offal of our sins — a method more conducive to mind control than finding felicity, let alone God. Instead, Traherne shows us how both Eden and the New Jerusalem are always already present and that it is simply a matter of allowing ourselves to see them, to enter them, to have them enter into us. As the twentieth century critic Helen White observed, "Above all, one is conscious in reading Traherne of the privilege of entering into the experience of a man to whom God and the Creation have come home in a peculiarly intimate and direct fashion. There is something of the freshness of the beginning of the world about Traherne. For he has seen for himself the reality of which he is writing."[24] It certainly is a privilege, but I don't think the priest Thomas Traherne

23   Robert Ellrodt, *Seven Metaphysical Poets: A Structural Study of the Unchanging Self* (Oxford: Oxford University Press, 2000), 178.
24   Helen C. White, *The Metaphysical Poets: A Study in Religious Experience* (New York: The Macmillan Company, 1936), 374.

would find satisfaction in focusing on himself. Far more than himself, he is interested in the spiritual welfare of his readers: that they should know that a way exists out of the madness of modernity and self-interest and that we can overcome our fallen egocentricity by entering the glorified egocentricity of Eden and the New Jerusalem: "I on the Earth did reign. / Within, without me, all was pure. / I must becom a Child again."[25]

---

25 "Innocence," stanza 5.

7

The Green Man and
the Invisible Country

FOR MAE

O NCE UPON A TIME, IN A SUMMERLAND
called The Late-Nineteen Hundreds, my wife and I
went to the Michigan Renaissance Festival accoutered
in festival attire and accompanied by our then-extant brood
(might have been three, might have been four or five—I'm not
good at keeping track), at least one of whom was probably in a
stroller. At one point in our festivality, we encountered a unique
character: The Green Man. This was an ingenious character and
even more ingenious costume. The figure looked not unlike the
ents from the Lord of the Rings films (long before they appeared),
but it was much less bulky—in fact, it was rather lithe. Through
a clever use of stilts and crutch-like appendages extending from
where the hands must have been, it stood at least ten-feet tall
and moved at an excruciatingly slow pace. I stood there dumb-
founded. After ten minutes or so of taking in the spectacle, my
wife and our easily-bored little ones wanted to move on, though
I stalled them as long as I could before finally acquiescing.

As we moved along in search of jousting and/or sword-
swallowing, my wife asked, "Why were you so into that thing?"
I told her the truth: "I've seen him before."

Only I didn't mean I'd seen this-guy-in-an-ingenious-costume-
at-the-Renaissance-Festival. I meant "The Green Man."

Allow me to explain.

In the mid-80s, while out for a picnic in the woods, I had
seen a figure very much like the one I'd encountered at the

festival. At least I thought I did. The figure I saw in the woods, though, or rather *figures* (there were more than one) seemed to travel at an even slower rate, more or less through the canopy of maple and oak trees around me. They were a bit smaller than the costumed figure, but very similar, only less "substantial." Imagine a walking nervous system, but replace the nerves with twigs and sticks and you'll get the idea. Of course, seeing such things is crazy. So I convinced myself my eyes were playing tricks on me. I never thought about it again until that moment at the festival.

One fall afternoon several years later as my wife was raking leaves in our yard, our eldest daughter, then probably three-years-old, asked her to stop what she was doing. "Those people," she said, pointing to the place in the garden where her mother had just cleared some leaves. My wife saw nothing, but our daughter was insistent and didn't want the people to be hurt. She's now almost twenty-five and still swears it really happened.

Years later, I found another daughter's makeshift booklet outside (she was about seven or eight at the time). It read:

> On the cover, in a circle, the title: **Fairys**
> Page 1: *Sientifec fairy Reaserch*
> — *when a baby laughs for the first time a fairy is born*

One day this same child showed up at the back door with a long-handled fishing net.

"What do you want?" I asked.

"Is this good for capturing things?" she said.

"Depends," I answered. "What kinds of things?"

"Fairies," she replied, very forthrightly.

I told her I thought it could work; it was worth a shot. She was not successful.

Of course, children often believe that fairies exist. We find it cute. When they don't grow out of it, we find them odd. But some never grow out of it. Some of these children grow up to be philosophers and theologians, which is perhaps not as surprising as one might think. Two that come immediately to mind are John Milbank and David Bentley Hart. I am sure there are others. Some, though, tend to hide this proclivity beneath a literary veneer — affirming J. R. R. Tolkien, C. S. Lewis, and even J. K. Rowling as imaginative explorers of the land of magic, but ultimately backing off from actually signing on the dotted line. Such a posture may be very convenient, but also a bit cowardly: a kind of aestheticism both disingenuous and patronizing. At best, I wonder if such individuals are simply hedging their bets and trying to cover their behinds. At worst, there might be something of infantilization at work there. Freud wasn't exactly a moron.

My grandfather, Michael Patrick Conlon, was born in Carrick-on-Shannon, Ireland in 1910 and died in Detroit in 1984. He was a burly redhead who worked in a factory, but, on some summer evenings when I was a child — prompted, no doubt, by Altes and Kessler's — he would tell his grandchildren stories of his childhood (or those he'd heard in childhood) concerning the invisible kingdom and its denizens. He was not one of those people given to fancy; but he knew these things were true.

Untold numbers of people claim to have seen into this kingdom, and in the early twentieth century it was still easy to collect their stories, though I imagine now such experiences are not nearly as common as they used to be. Unfortunately, positivistic psychology, science, and sociology dismissed these kinds of experiences as wish-fulfillment, or as the product of unintended ingestion of natural hallucinogens, or as a kind of atavistic primitivism. I never liked these kinds of explanations, which always seems to me examples of the kind of arrogant colonization Western intellectuals have yet to resist inflicting on peoples and cultures they deem inferior.

The Canadian philosopher Charles Taylor has written about the development of a "buffered self" that accompanied the rise of modernity and the Scientific Revolution and which cordoned Western people from a porosity to nature and a trust in realities not readily apparent to the five senses: realities such as fairies, of course, but also those concerning the subtle qualities of things (such as the Moon, relics, holy water, icons), not to mention angels, demons, even God. [1] The Scientific Revolution and the Reformation served as what Taylor calls "engines of disenchantment" made only more efficient by the Enlightenment and what followed: the Industrial Revolution, the Communist revolutions, and, perhaps most insidiously, the digital revolution. And don't even get me started on the Fourth Industrial Revolution.

But even to use words like "re-enchantment" betrays that we don't really accept these realities; that we're simply nostalgic for a cultural past that lives only in our memory. We are still outside of it, doomed by a Cartesian separation oppressing us, an affliction of our cultural patrimony.

This affliction troubles most Christians today. I am often puzzled by theologians and other Christian intellectuals and academics who resolutely affirm the Real Presence in the Eucharist, the efficacy of prayer, and the existence of God, but who get a little fuzzy in their assurance when it comes to angels and demons, not to mention the qualities of relics and holy water. And don't even mention fairies or green men. If the numinous exists, it cannot be only in the context of the Mass. Unfortunately, most of us are only porous (or pretend to be) on Sundays.

I think one of the best examples of a figure who can hold both Christian orthodoxy and folk belief in balance (with a little Roman paganism thrown in) is the seventeenth-century Anglican priest and poet Robert Herrick, whom I've written about in my book, The Incarnation of the Poetic Word. In his massive Hesperides and Noble Numbers, Herrick asserts the joy of parish life: a life that includes Christian piety as well as pagan revelry. In his unwieldy collection of verses, Herrick embraces the rosary as well as the maypole, the lares as well as the Holy Spirit, the annoying members of the parish as well as the beautiful maidens, the Virgin Mary as well as Queen Mab, the fairy kingdom as well as the Kingdom of God. The world

---

1   In A Secular Age (Cambridge, MA: Belknap Press, 2007).

he describes is a messy one, but open to all. And that is about as Christian as it gets. The fact that he published his book after being ejected from his living in Devonshire and used it as a stick to thrust in the eye of the tiresome Puritan killjoys who censured him makes it all the more delicious.

An important aspect of Herrick's book is that it also serves as a lament for a world that was passing away: the world of a faith life integrated with nature. Nowhere does he describe so directly this world he so loved as in "The Argument of his Book":

> I sing of brooks, of Blossomes, Birds, and Bowers,
> Of April, May, of June, and July-Flowers.
> I sing of May-poles, Hock-carts, Wassails, Wakes,
> Of Bride-grooms, Brides, and of their Bridall-cakes.
> I write of Youth, of Love, and have Accesse
> By these, to sing of cleanly-Wantonnesse.
> I sing of Dewes, of Raines, and piece by piece
> Of Balme, of Oyle, of Spice, and Amber-Greece.
> I sing of Times trans-shifting; and I write
> How Roses first came Red, and Lillies White.
> I write of Groves, of Twilights, and I sing
> The Court of Mab, and of the Fairie-King.
> I write of Hell; I sing (and ever shall)
> Of Heaven, and hope to have it after all. [2]

As the Scientific Revolution asserted its hegemony, as the Reformations (and Counter-Reformation) reduced the Church calendar to a shadow of its simultaneously cosmic/agrarian and divine character, and as enclosure laws and the march of a rapacious capitalism more and more removed people from the land and drove them into the squalor of the cities and the self-fulfilling prophecy of a dastardly social Darwinism, there was no room left for such a world. Such a world — of fasts, festivity, and divinity, of fairies, fertility, and fairs — is not efficient. It is not economically viable. Shareholders don't like it.

---

2 *The Poetical Works of Robert Herrick*, ed. L. C. Martin (Oxford: The Clarendon Press, 1956).

Our own world has no fasts to speak of, so it has no true festivity. It is hostile to both divinity and fertility. But it has its own fairies. Indeed, is not the internet a diabolical fairy Otherworld, a world of no material substance that nevertheless exists? Is not the posture of the person with a cellphone in his or her lap the same as the person in a state of contemplation? Do we not enter another world in just this way, whether in contemplative repose or by way of a screen? Is not the second of these a demonic parody of the former?

It seems to me that a connection to the natural world and its rhythms, to the wheel of the cosmos and the cycle of the liturgical year, is the anti-internet because it's the real internet: it opens us to what is real, the intertwined realms of the natural and the supernatural, and it helps us stay in touch with each other because it allows us to stay in touch with reality. In considering the sterile benefits of modernity at the beginning of the twentieth century, G. K. Chesterton saw the return to the land as a significant part of the return to sanity: "If we ever get the English back onto English land they will become again a religious people, if all goes well, a superstitious people. The absence from life of both the higher and lower forms of faith is largely due to a divorce from nature and the trees and clouds."[3] We could use some healthy superstition connected to nature instead of the unhealthy superstition of virtual reality by which our humanity has become so degraded.

What I am saying, then, is that the green man I saw (or didn't see) so long ago, the little people my daughter saw as a child, and that many of the thousands upon thousands (probably more like millions) of experiences others have had of the invisible realm throughout history are indicative of what I have called in another context *a poetic metaphysics*. And by "poetic" I do not mean less real than what we're accustomed to. On the contrary, I mean *more real* than what we're accustomed to.

---

3   Gilbert K. Chesterton, *Heretics* (New York: Dodd, Mead & Company, 1923), 101.

Such a world is not any more inconsistent with Christian belief than the internet is. Indeed, being mindful of even the possibility of such a world can certainly restore health to psyches affected in untold ways by the ravages of postmodernity so clearly made manifest in the utter madness so prevalent on social media and the internet. The digital revolution, like those before, cares nothing for human flourishing, but, like its antecedents, merely instrumentalizes human beings for other purposes. As Martin Heidegger told us so long ago, technology is never neutral.

At the first performance of J. M Barrie's *Peter Pan* on December 27th, 1904, no one knew what to expect when, after Tinkerbell's death, Peter asked the audience, "Do you believe in fairies? If you believe, wave your handkerchiefs and clap your hands!" An anxious Barrie had told the orchestra to be ready to lay down their instruments and clap their loudest when that moment came. But when it did come, the audience burst into such overwhelming applause that the actress playing Peter Pan burst into tears and had to leave the stage for a few moments to compose herself.

I don't think people are any different now. Only now, people are even more distanced from nature: that lack more than compensated for by their addictive involvement with their phones. They still desire a connection with the real, but look for it in exactly the wrong place.

I'm not suggesting everyone try to see fairies or the Green Man, or even to believe that such things exist. All I am saying is that there is more to the natural world than can be boiled down to an algorithm. As William Blake wrote, "We who dwell on Earth can do nothing of ourselves; everything is conducted by Spirits, no less than Digestion or Sleep."[4]

Those of us who go by the name Christian would do well to not confine the numinous to Sundays, for the Lord poured

---

4 From "To the Public" in *Jerusalem: The Emanation of the Giant Albion*.

out his Wisdom over all of nature (Sirach 1:9). God is a spirit, and he is to be worshipped in spirit and truth. And spirit is impervious to data or algorithms.

In the early twentieth century, there was a veritable fairy craze, an artifact of which is *Peter Pan*, a rousing success in both print and in the theatre — not to mention the early silent film version from 1924. Not only Barrie's work, but the discovery of the Cottingley Faeries who became *cause célèbre* in 1917 — even though most (but not all) of the photographs of fairies captured by two Yorkshire lassies were later admitted to have been faked — contributed to what was by that point a far-reaching cultural phenomenon. A little earlier, in the 1880s, a young William Butler Yeats had combed the libraries of England and the cottages and libraries of Ireland for folk and fairy tales of the Irish, later published in *Fairy and Folk Tales of the Irish Peasantry* (1888) and *Irish Fairy Tales* (1892), a research project which profoundly impacted his own poetry, as in "The Wanderings of Oisin" or "The Stolen Child" with its tragic and mournful refrain:

> Come away, O human child!
> To the waters and the wild
> With a faery, hand in hand.
> For the world's more full of weeping than you can
>   understand.

In the milieu of burgeoning industrialization and even World War I, the desire to recapture at least some of what was vanishing can clearly be seen in the period's widespread interest in fairies.

A scholarly dissertation on fairies was even undertaken during the first decade of the twentieth century by a young American, W. Y. Evans-Wentz, while at Oxford, later published in book form in 1911 as *The Fairy-Faith in Celtic Countries*. Evans-Wentz's book is to date the most comprehensive and rigorous exploration of the belief in fairies. Timing is everything, though, as finding a peasantry enmeshed in the world of nature and close to the invisible worlds would have been far easier in the days before the arrival of electricity and the radio, let alone multi-national corporations and the internet. Evans-Wentz collected much of the material for his book from interviewing the peasantry of Ireland, Scotland, Wales, The Isle of Man, Cornwall, and Brittany, and what he found among the disparate cultures had much in common, so much so that he proposes that "the evidence is so clear that little or no comment is necessary."[5] As he writes further:

> Most of the evidence also points so much in one direc-
> tion that the only verdict which seems reasonable is
> that the Fairy-Faith belongs to a doctrine of souls; that
> is to say, that Fairyland is a state or condition, realm or
> place, very much like, if not the same as, that wherein
> civilized and uncivilized men alike place the souls of
> the dead, in company with other invisible beings such
> as gods, daemons, and all sorts of good and bad spirits.
> Not only do both educated and uneducated Celtic seers
> so conceive Fairyland, but they go much further, and say
> that Fairyland actually exists as an invisible world within
> which the visible world is immersed like an island in an
> unexplored ocean, and that it is peopled by more species
> of living beings than this world, because incomparably
> more vast and varied in its possibilities.

Allow me to emphasize: this was at Oxford. Oxford University. Evans-Wentz's examiners at Oxford were the great Celticist Sir John Rhys and Andrew Lang, the much beloved collector of fairy- and folktales. I imagine he would be hard-pressed to find such congenial professors were he to undertake the project today, unless he could somehow bend his study to the will of theory. Thank God he worked when he did.

Among the interviews Evans-Wentz features in the book, one is presented as "An Irish Mystic's Testimony." We now know this mystic was the poet, artist, and social activist George William

---

5   W. Y. Evans-Wentz, *The Fairy-Faith in Celtic Countries* (1911; reprt., University Books, 1966), 18.

Russell, known better under the pseudonym A. E. To Russell's perception, the fairies, whom he calls by the Irish term the *Sidhe* or "the shining ones," exist in a *metaxu*, "the mid-world," which lies between the earth-world and the heaven-world. He also believed that these beings do not possess a sense of individuality as humans do. "Theirs is a collective life, so unindividualized and so calm that I might have more varied thoughts in five minutes than they would have in five years; and yet one feels an extraordinary purity and exaltation about their life. . . . A hive of bees has been described as a single organism with disconnected cells; and some of these tribes of shining beings seem to be little more than one being manifesting itself in many beautiful forms."[6] Russell was both a fine painter and a sensitive poet, and he captures something of the condition for seeing into the mid-world in his poem, "The Dream of the Children":

> The children were glad; it was lonely
>   To play on the hillside by day.
> "But now," they said, "we have only
>   To go where the good people stray."
>
> For all the hillside was haunted
>   By the faery folk come again;
> And down in the heart-light enchanted
>   Were opal-coloured men.
>   . . . .
> This golden breath was a madness
>   To set a poet on fire;
> And this was a cure for sadness,
>   And that the ease of desire.[7]

This is surely a description — and the fruit — of reverie.

One of the more fascinating studies of the invisible country prior to Evans-Wentz's magisterial study was the Rev. Robert Kirk's seventeenth century manuscript *The Secret Commonwealth*,

6 Ibid., 62–63.
7 A. E., *Collected Poems* (London: Macmillan and Co., 1931), lines 24–28, 45–48.

which Andrew Lang in the introduction to the edition he prepared calls "a kind of metaphysic of the Fairy world."[8] Kirk's book, like Evans-Wentz's, is a scholar's account, though, like his fellow investigator's, reflective of the scholarly conventions of his time. He simply collates the extant material pertinent to his research — which was considerable — and does so without condemnation or bias in a very matter-of-fact, methodical manner. Churchmen, especially rural churchmen like Kirk, connected and accustomed to the attitudes and thoughts of the peasantry, have been some of the more interested in these abstruse studies through the centuries; though with the disappearance of the peasantry, increasing urbanization and the, ahem, "sophistication" that comes with it have made such figures rare indeed.

I have often wondered why sightings into the invisible world, or at least interest in such sightings, have all but disappeared from the general cultural imaginary, though they lurk at the margins. When Evans-Wentz interviewed the then seventy-three-year-old Neil Colton of Donegal, the old gentleman remarked on the diminished population of the shining ones, saying, "These races were terribly plentiful a hundred years ago, and they'll come back again."[9] Did they? They certainly didn't go away entirely, as accounts of fairy sightings proliferated throughout the twentieth century, often given by children or by adults recounting experiences from childhood; but plenty of adults reported seeing the shining ones as well, not to mention my own account.[10] Nevertheless, there does seem to be a dearth of fairy sightings during postmodernity. Some would certainly argue that belief in fairies is inconsistent

---

8   Andrew Lang, Introduction to Robert Kirk, *The Secret Commonwealth of Elves, Fauns, and Fairies* (1893; reprt. Mineola, NY: Dover Publications, 2008), 15.

9   W. Y. Evans-Wentz, *The Fairy-Faith in Celtic Countries*, 73.

10   An exhaustive collection of such reports can be found in Marjorie T. Johnson's *Seeing Fairies: From the Lost Archives of the Fairy Investigation Society, Authentic Reports in Modern Times* (San Antonio, TX: Anomalist Books, 2014).

with modernity, let alone postmodernity; but people have also argued religious faith, and Christianity in particular, is inconsistent with modernity. I do not buy into these assumptions.

There are, to be sure, many people who claim to see into the secret commonwealth. Just a simple internet search will lead to dozens, if not hundreds, of links that promise instruction in fairy communication, their language often sounding like the spiritual-but-not-religious version of the hard sell: "Read on, fairy lovers, to learn how to see fairies in the garden and communicate with the Fair Folk of your local area!" I am skeptical of such claims. It's not that I don't believe in the existence of the fair folk; it's just that I have a hard time getting past the cultivated personas (or avatars) that often accompany such promises and the almost requisite alt-spirituality cosplay that goes along with them, replete with flowing skirts, thumb-rings, and scarves. Lots and lots of scarves. This is a far cry from the rustic and unlettered farmers and cottagers with whom Yeats and Evans-Wentz spoke. Not that the cosplayers are without merit: clearly they hunger for something of which our culture deprives them. I understand their hunger for a world re-enchanted. I simply don't think it requires a costume.

Of course, the disenchantment the faeish cosplayers attempt to remedy is at its core also a lament for the exile of God, of angels, and of the presence of the dead in the era of technocracy and transhumanism. In that, they are not unlike the Romantics who rejected the antiseptic and icy values of the Enlightenment and embraced the possibilities of a more human civilization; and they would, without a doubt, hope with Yeats that this condition may come to pass and "an age of imagination, of emotion, of moods, of revelation . . . come in its place."[11] But the problem the Romantics faced is the same, in essence, that we see in fairy cosplay: the dissipation into Gothic silliness. Enter the Goth vampires and the fairies that look like Barbie

11   William Butler Yeats, "The Body of Father Christian Rosencrux (1895)" in *Essays and Introductions* (New York: The Macmillan Company, 1961), 197.

dolls. This is what happens with a spirituality not moored by a relationship to Creation and grounded in the Real.

I have often wondered, typically when I'm working in the garden on my farm, how it is that the denizens of the secret commonwealth are so seldom seen when compared to times past. Part of it, as I have noted, is surely due to the disenchantment of modernity. The hubris of modernity seems impervious to self-reflection. All cultures throughout all times save the last two-hundred years have held to the existence of the invisible worlds, and many still do, though that belief in an invisible world is more and more transferred to the magical world of the internet and the more immediate satisfactions to fancy it offers.

For example, Paul Devereux relates the story of German cultural anthropologist Christian Rätsch, who in order to understand the lifeway of a Lacandon tribe in southern Mexico entered into it as a participant and not as the "impartial observer" so lauded by Western academic standards. Rätsch learned their language, and the Indians taught him how to hunt, gather, and farm according to their ways. One day, when Rätsch was keeping guard over the village corn crop in order to drive away predators, a bird landed on the branch of a tree nearby which he saw fit for a meal and shot. When he went to retrieve the bird, he was in for a surprise. "There was not the corpse of a bird;" he said, "there was not a single feather! Then I looked up into the tree and there was not even the branch!" When he told the village elder what had happened, the man laughed and told him that such things happened sometimes, and that it was just the jungle spirits teasing him.[12] I'm sure they were.

Despite the epistemological and social conventions of modernity, I also wonder how its own paraphernalia itself might be destructive to the secret commonwealth, or at least our ability to perceive it. For one thing, electricity may pose a hindrance,

---

12   Paul Devereux, *Re-Visioning the Earth: A Guide to Opening the Healing Channels between Mind and Nature* (New York: Fireside/Simon & Schuster, 1996), 29.

particularly the power grid that almost invisibly strikes its lines over the land. It might negatively impact the invisible realm, and it might also impact our own capacities of perception. And one can only speculate about the impact of 5G towers and the almost numberless satellites constantly filling the air with their silent presence and radiations. This is to say nothing of plastic, the bane of Creation. While finding a stray shard of plastic while weeding my garden, I often wonder if the fairies are allergic to it and that's why they've been disappearing. Plastics only arrived in the early 20th century (I think of the wonderful scene in the motion picture *The Graduate* when a well-meaning middle-classer has one word of advice for the graduate, Benjamin: "Plastics"), and, while correlation doesn't necessarily imply causation, I have nevertheless wondered how the two phenomena might be related. Plastic has certainly contributed to the disenchantment of the world in other ways. What I offer is speculation, of course, but I think what I speak here possesses at the very least a poetic — that is to say a greater — truth.

Truth often arrives by mysterious means. For example, a series of mysterious events marked my grandfather's gradual demise and eventual death from lung cancer in 1987. I was working as a musician by night and had a day job running an offset printing press, while my mother worked in the office next door. While my grandfather was ill and in the hospital, his sister Mae died. She was one year his senior and besides him the only of their many siblings (a floating population somewhere between nine and thirteen, including fosterlings and cousins) to have emigrated to the United States. Grandpa's condition was so precarious the family decided not to tell him she'd died until he had more strength. The morning after Mae died, my grandmother went to visit him.

"Mae was here," he told her.

"I don't think that's possible, Mike," she answered.

"Mae was here, and she sat right in that chair where you're sitting now. We talked about Ireland. She mentioned John."

Their brother John, my grandfather's closest brother, had died sixty years previously in Ireland of influenza, and my grandfather always felt he was to blame. His siblings were calling my grandfather home to the Brighter Country.

A few months later, on the day before St. Patrick's Day, as it turns out, I was at work printing a run of fliers. All of a sudden, my press started shooting streams of paper into the air, almost like $8\frac{1}{2} \times 11$ confetti. When I shut off the machine to investigate, I looked next to me and saw my mother, her eyes full of tears.

"Grandpa's dead," she told me.

It was as if something prompted the press to mark my grandfather's passing. And not only in Michigan. When my grandmother called Grandpa's sister Kitty in England to tell her the news, Kitty said she knew someone had died. A picture fell off the wall earlier that day, a sure sign. I'm not sure exactly who the actors of these events were, but I do know that they belong to some sort of secret commonwealth, a demesne in which we all participate, though we don't often acknowledge or recognize it. "Coincidence" is not an adequate explanation.

J. R. R. Tolkien wrote of such a country in his saga of Middle Earth, and I'm sure he had in mind the vanishing of the fairies in his mythopoesis. The elves in his mythos, exhausted by war and toil, begin to leave Middle Earth for the Undying Lands:

> In those days there was a great building of ships upon the shores of the Western Sea; and thence in many a fleet the Eldar set sail into the West, and came never back to the lands of weeping and of war. And the Vanyar returned beneath their white banners, and were borne in triumph to Valinor; but their joy in victory was diminished, for they knew that those jewels could not be found or brought together again unless the world be broken and remade. [13]

---

13   J. R. R. Tolkien, *The Silmarillion*, ed. Christopher Tolkien (Boston: Houghton Mifflin Company, 1977), 254.

Not all the elves leave, of course, as any reader of Tolkien well knows, but their presence in Middle Earth is as fragile and tenuous as a quince blossom in a late frost. So it is with the shining ones in our world. Perhaps the devastation of the World Wars, Hiroshima, and the never-ending cycle of destruction through the twentieth and, alas, twenty-first centuries, events that have wreaked so much havoc on Creation, have demoralized them beyond staying. For the world's more full of weeping than they can understand. Nevertheless, I believe with Tolkien that they can be found and brought together if the world be broken and remade. Broken it is, we cannot deny. We have only to begin the charm of remaking. But we have to find the words, the images, the stories, and the songs — yes! the songs! — that call them back to our world. And by doing so, we will also return ourselves to the world. For their story — and their fate — is ours.

8
Filling the Empty Signifier
THREE MEDITATIONS
ON THE GRAIL

It has to be confessed that we have come forth from a pro-
longed study of the Grail Critical Apparatus with empty hands.
$\sim$: Arthur Edward Waite[1]

THE FISHER KING

If one story has haunted me, remained ever-present to me
over the past thirty-five years or so, it is the story of Wolfram
von Eschenbach's *Parzival* (c. 1210). Unlike the Galahad of *Le
Conte de Graal*, a boring, already-perfect figure who gets the Grail
and evaporates like monastic froth into the ethers of a celibate
dreamscape, Wolfram's Parzival starts off as a complete goof: a
bumbling teenager who stumbles into knighthood almost by
accident — and even when he's made a knight, it still takes
him a long time to figure out how to *be* one. As he discovers,
it's not just a matter of wearing some knightly swag. Parzival's
hamartia resides in the fact that he heeds advice far too literally and without any idea of context: first that of his mother,
Herzeloyde, and then that of his mentor, Gurnemanz. When
Herzeloyde, even though she has tried to shield her son from
any notion of knighthood, agrees to let her son go off to seek
it, among other things, she tells him, "Whenever you can win a
lady's ring and greeting, take it — it will rid you of the dumps.
Waste no time, but kiss and embrace her."[2] Following this advice,

---

1   Arthur Edward Waite, *The Holy Grail: The Galahad Quest in Arthurian
Literature* (1933; rprt. Montana: Kessinger, 1993), 479.
2   Wolfram von Eschenbach, *Parzival*, trans. A. T. Hatto (New York: Penguin, 1980), 75.

he basically accosts the first woman he meets, obedient as he is stupid, and takes her ring in the bargain, only pausing to say "God be with you! — That's what my mother told me to say." [3] Though he breaks the boy of the habit of talking about what his mother told him all the time, Gurnemanz doles out some equally good/bad advice, though with the best of intentions: "Do not ask many questions." Later, when Parzival encounters the graciousness and suffering of Anfortas, the Fisher King (unbeknownst to Parzival, his uncle) while in the presence of the Holy Grail, his heart burns to ask Anfortas why he suffers. But he doesn't. As a result, Anfortas is condemned to more suffering and Parzival to aimless (or so it would seem) wandering.

I can identify with Parzival's bumbling. I think we all can. But more and more, as I get older, my attention turns to the suffering of the Fisher King.

As I survey the wasteland of Western culture and its current nadir, I cannot but help think that we are all simultaneously the bumbling fool and the suffering king. We do so many hurtful and stupid things, not because our mothers told us to, but certainly in obedience to some variety of superego or egregore. We do what we think we are supposed to do. And we are usually wrong. Likewise, the pains we bear in silence have never healed, though we wait upon the kindness of strangers or hope for a savior at the horizon. Anfortas was once like Parzival, once *was* a Parzival, but his overreaching caused him to be wounded: a wound to the thigh, signifying impotence. Our social media harangues — are they not evidence of a fear of impotence? The great Terry Gilliam film The Fisher King beautifully illustrates how we can be both Parzival and Anfortas. Who's really wounded in this film, Jack or Perry? Who really needs healing? Who doesn't?

The good news is that healing is possible. On Parzival's second visit to the Grail Castle, he asks the question: "Uncle, what is it that ails you?" He receives no answer. But Anfortas is healed,

3   Ibid., 77.

nonetheless. This theme of healing inhabits many tellings of the Grail story — that of the Indiana Jones franchise no less than Richard Wagner's *Parsifal* (which certainly has some Galahad-like overtones). Perhaps one of the most intriguing modern treatments of the story (not to mention Eric Rohmer's *Percivale le Gallois*) is Hans-Jürgen Syberberg's 1982 film of Wagner's opera.

In Syberberg's treatment, both a teenaged boy (played by Michael Kutter) and a young woman (Karin Krick) play Parzival. Through such daring casting, Syberberg paints a picture of psychic integration, or what C. G. Jung would call the *coniunctio oppositorum* (the conjunction of opposites), the interiorization of the feminine into the male psyche and the interiorization of the masculine into the feminine. Our culture has failed to accomplish this task for far too long, and it is a significant source of our suffering.

THE ONCE AND FUTURE CHURCH

The legend of King Arthur (also called The Matter of Britain) ends in tragedy: Arthur dies in battle against Mordred, his son begotten through incest, after having lost his wife Guinevere and best friend Sir Lancelot to each other. It is a tale of sexual sin: sometimes unconscious, sometimes in the full light of consciousness and volition. Both have disastrous consequences.

As Arthur lay dying on the field of Camlann he bids his knight Sir Bedivere to dispose of the sword Excalibur, the symbol of Arthur's power and, inversely, his impotence (he was unable to produce an heir by his rightful spouse). As Sir Thomas Malory describes it:

> "Therefore," seyde kynge Arthur unto sir Bedwere, "take thou here Excalibur, my good swerde, and go wyth it to yondir watirs syde; and whan thou commyst there, I charge the throw my swerde in that water, and com agayne and telle me what thou syeste there." "My lorde," seyde sir Bedwere, "youre commaundement shall be done, and lyghtly brynge you worde agayne."

147

So sir Bedwere departed. And by the way he behylde that noble swerde, and the pomell and the hauffte was all precious stonys. And than he seyde to hymselff: "If I throw thys ryche swerde in the water, thereof shall never com good, but harme and losse." And than sir Bedwere hyd Excalybur under a tre, and so as sone as he myght, he cam agayne unto the kynge and seyde he had bene at the watir and had throwen the swerde into the watir.

"What sawe thou there?" seyde the kynge.

"Sir," he seyde, "I saw nothyng but wavis and wyndys."

"That ys untruly seyde of the," seyde the kynge. "And therefore go thou lyghtly agayne, and do my commaundement; as thou arte to me lyff and dere, spare nat, but throw hit in."

Than sir Bedwere returned agayne and toke the swerde in hys honde; and yet hym thought synne and shame to throw away that noble swerde. And so effte he hyd the swerde and returned agayne and tolde to the kynge that he had bene at the watir and done hys commaundement.

"What sawist thou there?" seyde the kynge.

"Sir," he seyde, "I saw nothyng but the watirs wap and wawys wanne."

"A, traytour unto me and untrew," seyde kyng Arthure, "now hast thou betrayed me twyse! Who wolde wene that thou that hast bene to me so leve and dere, and also named a noble knyghte, that thou wolde betray me for the ryches of thys swerde? But now go agayne lyghtly; for thy long tarryynge putteth me in grete jouperté of my lyff, for I have takyn colde. And but if thou do now as I bydde the, if ever I may se the, I shall sle the myne owne hondis; for thou woldist for my rych swerde se me dede."

Than sir Bedwere departed and wente to the swerde and lyghtly toke it up, and so he wente to the watirs syde. And there he bounde the gyrdyll aboute the hyltis, and threw the swerde as farre into the watir as he myght. And there cam an arme and an honde above the watir, and toke hit and cleyght hit, and shoke it thryse and braundysshed, and than vanysshed with the swerde in the watir.

So sir Bedwere cam agayne to the kynge, and tolde hym what he saw.

"Alas," seyde the kynge, "helpe me hens, for I drede me I have taryed over longe."

Than sir Bedwere toke the kynge upon hys bak and so wente with hym to that watir syde. And whan they were there, evyn faste by the banke hoved a lyttl barge wyth many fayre ladyes in hit, and amonge hem all was a quene, and all they had blak hodis. And all they wepte and shryked whan they saw kynge Arthur.

"Now put me into that barge," seyed the kynge.

And so he ded softly, and there resceyved him three ladyes with grete mournyng. And so they sette hem downe, and in one of their lappis kynge Arthure layde hys hede. And than that quene seyde:

"A, my dere brothir! Why have ye taryed so longe from me? Alas, thys wounde on your hede hath caught overmuch cold!"

And anone they rowed fromward the londe, and sir Bedwere behylde all tho ladyes go frowarde hym. Than sir Bedwere cryed and seyde,

"A, my lorde Arthur, what shall becom of me, now ye go frome me and leve me here alone amonge myne enemyes?"

"Comfort thyselff," seyde the kynge, "and do as well as thou mayste, for in me ys no truste for to truste in. For I muste into the vale of Avylyon to hele me of my grevous wounde. And if thou here never more of me, pray for my soule!"

But ever the quene and ladyes wepte and shryked, that hit was pité to hyre. And as sone as sir Bedwere had loste the syght of the barge, he wepte and wayled, and so toke the foreste and so wente all that nyght. [4]

---

4   Sir Thomas Malory, *Works*, ed. Eugene Vinaver, 2nd ed. (Oxford: Oxford University Press, 1971), 715–16.

Arthur's situation here is as that of the historical Church at this moment in time. Malory's denouement, however, is ambiguous:

> Yet som men say in many partys of Inglonde that kynge Arthure ys nat dede, but had by the wyll of oure Lorde Jesu into another place; and men say that he shall come agayne, and he shall wynne the Holy Crosse. Yet I woll not say hit shall be so, but rather I wolde say: here in thys worlde he changed hys lyff. But many men say that there ys wrytten upon his tombe thys:

> HIC JACET ARTHURUS,
> REX QUONDAM,
> REXQUE FUTURUS. [5]

In Malory's telling, the demise of the Round Table is anticipated long in advance and Arthur's knights embark upon the Quest of the Holy Grail as a way to avoid it. Clearly, the chalice is a supreme symbol of the Eucharist, of the regenerative Blood of Christ, and true *communio*. But also, as others have noted, this quest for the chalice is in many ways a quest for the feminine, an attempt to find psychic balance in a world over-dominated by the masculine. Here, too, is an image of the historical Church at our moment.

Some say the Church is not dead, nor can ever die, though it most certainly wanders in the Wasteland. I will venture no predictions, offer no diagnoses, other than to say that to win the Holy Cross, to win the Holy Vessel, it is incumbent in this world that one changes one's life.

> Son of man,
> You cannot say, or guess, for you know only
> A heap of broken images, where the sun beats,
> And the dead tree gives no shelter, the cricket no relief,
> And the dry stone no sound of water. [6]

---

5 Ibid., 717.
6 T. S. Eliot, "The Wasteland," lines 20–24, from T. S. Eliot, *The Complete Poems and Plays, 1909–1950* (New York: Harcourt, Brace & World, Inc., 1958).

THE EMPTY SIGNIFIER

I think the time has come to admit that what is called "the Holy Grail" is some variety of empty signifier or glittering generality. I know this is, in a way, "a hard saying," but, nevertheless, the time has come. But this is not to say that I don't think the Grail exists.

If we survey the Grail literature that arose during the late-medieval period, it quickly becomes apparent that exactly what kind of artifact the Grail is is really anyone's guess. We know the candidates: stone, altar, platter, lost jewel from Lucifer's crown, and the popular choice, the chalice used at the Last Supper. The *lapsit exillis* (a term likewise lacking in semantic stability) is also a red herring.

Therefore, the meaning of the Grail is forever deferred. Like the Messiah, it awaits always at the horizon: a horizon we have yet to attain. This notion preoccupied Jacques Derrida in the latter half of his career as a philosopher, and what he says regarding the (non)arrival of the Messiah is just as applicable as the search for the Grail:

> There is a possibility that my relation to the Messiah is this: I would like him to come, I hope that he will come, that the other will come, as other, for that would be justice, peace, and revolution — because in the concept of messianicity there is revolution — and at the same time, I am scared. I do not want what I want and I would like the coming of the Messiah to be infinitely postponed, and there is this desire in me.[7]

The intimations we have of the Grail likewise contain both hope and anxiety. We know it's good. We know it's holy. We just don't know what it is.

Because of its instability as a symbol, the Grail can become the receiver for human imagination (certainly the strength of

7   John D. Caputo (ed.), *Deconstruction in a Nutshell: A Conversation with Jacques Derrida*, 2nd ed. (New York: Fordham, University Press, 1996), 24–25.

the Grail literature — from the medieval origins to the sub-
limity of Wagner's *Parsifal* and the slapstick of Monty Python).
But with the imaginal license imparted by this floating signifier
comes the potential for danger. That is, as French philosopher
Jean-Luc Marion has described the human capacity for symbol-
making, the Grail can become either an icon or an idol. [8] As
an icon, it allows the divine to shine through it (however we
might imagine that divine); as an idol, it, like a mirror, reflects
our own desires (and egos) back to us. For many, I suspect, the
idolatry of the Grail unfolds in the way of the spiritual mega-
lomania of which Valentin Tomberg warns — repeatedly — in
Meditations on the Tarot (a warning which also appears, in a very
humorous way, in *The Chymical Wedding of Christian Rosenkreutz*).
I have met more than a few self-appointed "Initiates" or "Grail
Knights" in my time. As have we all.

The Grail Initiates and Knights of my acquaintance have
one thing in common: a very clearly defined notion of what
the Grail is (and what it is not). When questioned, they tend
to get very defensive or dismissive. These kinds of responses
could be, I admit, due to the fact that they really are Initiates
or Grail Knights. But, as any psychotherapist would say, such
defensiveness often indicates neurosis or even psychosis. I, for
my part, have chosen to eschew both initiation and psychosis.

As a rule, I tend to avoid such a hardened conceptual life.
History is littered with the ruins of grand schemes. Furthermore,
it seems to me that the spiritual world is much more characterized by fluidity than it is by rigidity. *Spiritus definitionem
abhoret.* Things change, transform, spiral, descend and ascend
in the spiritual world. They are never found twice in the same
place or same way.

And so it is with the Grail. My own intuitions and experiences tell me that, while the Grail is One, it is not one thing. I am
happy with the Grail as chalice and the Eucharistic implications

---

8   In his book *God without Being: Hors-Texte*, trans. Thomas A. Carlson
(Chicago: University of Chicago Press, 1991).

such an iconography embodies. Likewise am I at home with the Grail as platter, stone, or jewel from Lucifer's crown: so much poetic fertility lies in the Grail mythos that to choose one paradigm over another really works as a kind of betrayal of the Grail. And even though I prefer the Perceval/Parzival of Chrétien and Wolfram (somehow I have sympathy with a guy who screws up *everything* the first time) and have an inner revulsion for Galahad (kind of a combination of Captain America and a cherub; someone who never made a mistake in his life), I am comfortable with those who, like Charles Williams and A. E. Waite, look to Galahad as the Grail hero *par excellence* — just don't force me to drink from that cup.

More and more, however, the Grail for me has come to bear a deep resonance with both the earth itself and with the Eternal Feminine. This has less to do with Jessie Weston's project of applying *The Golden Bough* to the Grail mythos (as much as I enjoyed her book once upon a time) as it is to my experience as a biodynamic farmer and theologian. I have always been deeply moved by Rudolf Steiner's insight that the moment the Blood of Christ touched the earth on Golgotha the entire planet was given the capacity for new life; that it was saved from death. Likewise, I cherish Steiner's description of the moon filling with light prior to Easter as an image of the Grail: "At the Easter festival, therefore, everyone can see this picture of the Holy Grail."[9] I look for it every year and have taught my children to look for it.

Steiner's insights concerning the relationship of the Holy Blood and the Grail to Easter are given even deeper import by the Russian Orthodox priest Sergius Bulgakov's considerations of the Grail. For Bulgakov, like many commentators on the mythos, the Grail is intimately related to the Eucharist, but it is just as much related to the earth:

---

9   Rudolf Steiner, *The Mysteries of the Holy Grail: From Arthur and Parzival to Modern Initiation*, ed. Matthew Barton (Forrest Row, UK: Rudolf Steiner Press, 2010), 46.

The image of the Holy Grail, in which the holy blood of Christ is kept, expresses precisely the idea that, even though the Lord ascended in His honorable flesh to heaven, the world received His holy relic in the blood and water that flowed out of His side; and the chalice of the Grail is the ciborium and repository of this relic. *And the whole world is the chalice of the Holy Grail.* The Holy Grail is inaccessible to veneration; in its holiness it is hidden in the world from the world. However, *it exists in the world as an invisible power, and it becomes visible, appears to pure hearts who are worthy of its appearance.*[10]

Even though I appreciate the poetic image of Joseph of Arimathea catching the Holy Blood in the chalice of the Last Supper as Christ hung from the Cross, the picture Bulgakov offers here seems not only more true, but more necessary to life in the present. The center of ecology lies herein, in this picture of sacredness and regeneration, and not, as many contemporary environmentalists would have us believe, in encouraging feelings of shame, fear, and self-loathing. No one can be shamed or frightened into saving the world. Only love can bestow that kind of courage. I'm not a biodynamic farmer because I feel an urgency to save the world from the evils of men: I'm a farmer because it's the closest I can get to working with the Holy Blood that permeates the soil, however homeopathic the dose.

This picture of the Grail abiding in the world, I think, is an important one for us to carry. In the Galahad cycle, for instance, the Grail disappears from this plane (as does Galahad) and leaves behind sorrow and disillusionment (an understanding that permeates both Malory and Tennyson). Emma Jung and Marie-Louise von Franz, in their psychological exegesis, even implicate the Perceval/Parzival stream in this melancholy response, and wisely. "Perceval should not have taken himself into the seclusion of the Grail Castle," they write:

---

10 Sergius Bulgakov, *The Holy Grail and the Eucharist*, trans. Boris Jakim (Hudson, NY: Lindisfarne Books, 1997), 33. My emphasis.

In order to remain in the picture, he should have brought
the Grail to the Round Table, so that instead of the Spirit
being divorced from the world, the world would have
been impregnated by the Spirit.[11]

It is interesting that such a spirit-matter dichotomy infiltrates
so much of the Grail literature, as if spirit and matter were
separate realities and not aspects of the same reality. Nevertheless, what Jung and von Franz describe here is very much
how medieval Christianity in general, and the Galahad mythos
in particular (colored, as it is, by Albigensian and Cistercian
anxieties about sex and fertility), reified such a dichotomy.
Spiritual and psychological health would dictate that the Grail,
as Steiner and Bulgakov intuited, should remain with the earth.
The Grail's abiding on/in the earth also bears sophiological
implications as it opens a way for us to understand Creation
in a more complete way.

Despite the very masculine milieu of knighthood, the
Grail mythos also evokes images of what philosopher and
psychoanalyst Julia Kristeva describes as a "feminine genius."
Perceval/Parzival, for example, is raised by his mother away
from knighthood, and women are integral to his journey to
self-awareness. Indeed, when he first appears before the Grail,
Parzival is described by Wolfram as wearing the mantle of
Repanse de Schoye, clearly an image of the protection of sacred
femininity, and the hero doesn't even know his own name
until it is revealed to him by Sigune. Prior to the feminine
bestowal of his ego, we might say, Parzival is unequipped to
achieve the Grail (Gurnemanz's advice, need I remind anyone, proves unintentionally disastrous). Significantly, Kristeva
locates this feminine genius "as arising from the *loving singularity* discovered by Christianity."[12] During the High Middle

11   Emma Jung and Marie-Louise von Franz, *The Grail Legend*, trans. Andrea
Dykes (Boston: Sigo Press, 1986), 389.
12   Julia Kristeva, *This Incredible Need to Believe*, trans. Beverley Bie Brahic
(New York: Columbia University Press, 2009), 33.

Ages, in addition to the Grail mythos, we can see this loving singularity in relation to the feminine in Dante, in the rosary, and in *Brautmystik*. Closer to our own time, we can find it in psychoanalysis and Sophiology.

In their important book on the Grail legend, Emma Jung and Marie-Louise von Franz consider the feminine in relationship to the masculinity of the Holy Trinity. In their meditation, they see the Evil One as an unaccounted fourth in the quaternary completing the Father, Son, and Holy Spirit, but the Devil gives way to the Virgin Mary/Grail as a figure of redeemed evil: for the Grail stories are nothing if not meditations on the problem of evil and its transfiguration. "Even when the quaternary schema is arranged as overleaf with the Grail vessel (as substitute for the Mother of God)" they write,

> rather than the Devil added to the Trinity as the Fourth..., this does not dispose of the problem of evil. For, like the body of Mary, the Grail is something individual and material and thus also attracts the problem of evil to itself, because it too reaches down into the reality of earthly humanity. [13]

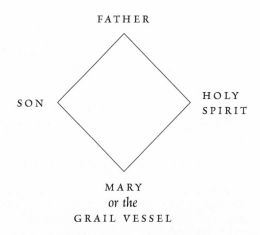

Figure 6: Diagram from Jung and von Franz

---

13   Emma Jung and Marie-Louise von Franz, *The Grail Legend*, 341.

The Book of Revelation attests to the same imagination:

> Now a great sign appeared in heaven: a woman clothed
> with the sun, with the moon under her feet, and on her
> head a garland of twelve stars. Then being with child, she
> cried out in labor and in pain to give birth.
>
> And another sign appeared in heaven: behold, a great,
> fiery red dragon having seven heads and ten horns, and
> seven diadems on his heads. His tail drew a third of the
> stars of heaven and threw them to the earth. And the
> dragon stood before the woman who was ready to give
> birth, to devour her Child as soon as it was born. (12:1–4)

For Bulgakov, the quaternary is filled/fulfilled in Sophia (and
he was censured by the Russian Orthodox Church for saying
so). The Trinity, according to Bulgakov, is mirrored in Sophia
(who simultaneously manifests herself in the Virgin Mary).[14]
Sophia, furthermore, inheres within Creation as a "unifying
force . . . cosmourgic potency. . . . She is the life of the world."[15]
An invisible stream, we can say, connects Sophia and the Holy
Blood which regenerated the earth at Golgotha. But here the
conceptual realm and the realm of logic break down and are
no longer of use: we enter the realm of poetic metaphysics.
Indeed, this is in every way a sacramental reality.

The Eternal Feminine inhabits this imaginal realm of poetic
metaphysics. As Kristeva says of the feminine genius, "thinking, for women, cannot be shut off from carnal sensoriality:
the metaphysical body/soul dichotomy is, in these women,
unbearable; they describe thought as physical happiness, *eros*
for them is not discernable from *agape* and vice versa."[16] My
experience as a husband, father, farmer, poet, and musician

---

14   Sergei Bulgakov, *Sophia, the Wisdom of God: An Outline of Sophiology*, trans.
Patrick Thompson, O. Fielding Clarke, and Xenia Braikevitc, rev. (Hudson,
NY: Lindisfarne Press, 1993), 37.

15   Sergius Bulgakov, *The Bride of the Lamb*, trans. Boris Jakim (Grand
Rapids, MI: William B. Eerdmans Publishing Company, 2002), 80.

16   Julia Kristeva, *This Incredible Need to Believe*, 39.

whispers to me that what Kristeva here describes as a feminine attribute is not unknown to men, and I think her intuition points to the key for finding the Grail in our day.

What we have here, then, are two images: of the Grail and of the Blood that fills it, of Sophia and Christ. Though I think the Gnostic mythos concerning Sophia is mostly wrong, it is true that she has been lost to humanity, entrapped in darkness — but not due to any mistakes she made. Unfortunately, feminist incursions into culture have transmogrified (literally in some cases) into a masculinization of the feminine, as if masculinity were the endgame of both evolution and feminism. Sophia can find no room in such a paradigm. However, if we awaken to the sophianic implicit in Creation (and creation), Sophia awakens. But, to be more accurate, Sophia does not need awakening. We do.

Arise.

9

The Rosary of
the Philosopher

Hear us, O Lord, from heaven thy dwelling place.

In the beginning was the Rose, and the Rose was with God.

The darkness of the cave. Three queens and fifty maidens. He nurses from the breast of a virgin.

ROSA. Rose. *Rosaceæ*. A large genus of shrubs, mostly prickly, often more or less scandent, native mostly in the north temp. zone, and furnishing many ornamental subjects: lvs. alternate, commonly pinnate: fls. white, yellow or red, solitary or in corymbs, prevailing in early summer: fr. a hip, archenes inclosed in a fleshy, nearly closed hollow receptacle, usually red. The species of Rosa can be accurately determined only from full technical descriptions; at this place some of the main horticultural features may be indicated. For cult see Rose.

Hear us, O Lord, from heaven thy dwelling place.

"I had scarcely closed my eyes before the apparition of a woman began to arise from the middle of the sea with so lovely a face that the gods themselves would have fallen down in adoration of it. First the head, then the whole shining body gradually emerged and stood before me poised on the surface of the waves. Yes, I will try to describe this transcendent vision, for though human speech is poor and limited, the Goddess herself will perhaps inspire me with poetic imagery sufficient to convey some slight inkling of what I saw."

Hear us, O Lord, from heaven thy dwelling place.

You prayed with the Beloved in the church of the Franciscans beneath the gaze of the Woman made of dark wood. Surrounded by apple orchards, gardens, a grove of pines, and crows.

In the story, the Holy One gives his devotee a rose and a lily. From the rose the disciple derives all fruits, from the lily all grains.

You remember the house in the city: the knot garden, the potager, the espaliered apples. The roses: climbers, ice white and blood red, that enveloped and enchanted the gazebo. You buried the placentas of your daughter and son at their roots.

Eleanor Farjeon falling asleep with her chaplet in her hands, the cerulean beads of blue, every night until the last awakening.

You make a metheglin flavored with rose petals to drink at the burning of the world.

The nearly closed, hollow receptacle. The cave.

You wear your chaplet under your clothes: the beads discolored by sweat, the pendant worn smooth by rubbing against your heart. Who, if you cried out, would hear you among the angels' hierarchies? Who?

"Hence when you look up and see the host, just freed from the hive, floating towards the starry sky through the clear summer air — when you marvel at the dark cloud trailing down the wind — mark it well; they are ever in quest of sweet waters and leafy coverts. Here scatter the scents I prescribe — bruised balm, and the honeywort's lowly herb; raise a tinkling sound, and shake the Mighty Mother's cymbals round about. Of themselves will they settle on the scented resting places; of themselves, after their wont, will hide far within their cradling cells."

You cut down the oak, you said, for firewood, though you really wanted to release the white hawthorn from the darkness.

Come into my garden.

Hear us, O Lord, from heaven thy dwelling place.

Covered with mud, bloodied, disfigured by torture, he handed a child a chaplet made of cord. The scaffold. The spectacle of too much weight.

Novalis in Dresden. Novalis at Sophie's grave. The children in the clouds. The Comforter.

"Si vis, quem optas in praedicando fructum, meum praedica psalterium."

You dump the rotting carcasses of dead bees into a cart, then give them to the fire where they audibly hiss. They bequeath you their stores which you eat with the bread of sorrow.

Perpetua's bowl of milk. The smiling shepherd.

"Rose, oh reiner Widerspruch, Lust, niemandes Schlaf zu sein unter soviel Lidern."

That year we had both frost and flooding in May, drought in June, and frost again in September. The Year of Plague.

Bulgakov, despondent, lost, weeping in Dresden before the Eternal Mother who calls him out of darkness.

"I would lack respect for the truth if I did not say that the *effort* of the rosary-prayer founded on *suffering* makes it a powerful means — sometimes all-powerful — in sacred magic."

In the grave of the night, awakened by the moon and the wind, you pray the beads of your fingers. Sorrow is a garden.

Hear us, O Lord, from heaven thy dwelling place.

"Thou unbegun and everlasting Wisdom, the which in thyself art the sovereign-substantial Firsthood, the sovereign Goddess, and the sovereign Good."

Your wife dreams of a woman mantled in blue, holding a shepherd's staff and guiding a herd of white horses through a valley. Their hooves thunder in waves as they rush up the hills and down again. She awakes in labor.

"A garden enclosed is my sister, my bride: a spring shut up, a fountain sealed."

The nearly closed hollow cave. Three queens and fifty maidens.

"But now the new Queen is born from out of the Sun, and brings Sun-light with her own body into the hive: now the bees become — I should like to say — clairvoyant with their little eyes. They cannot endure this light of the new Queen. The whole host of them prepares to swarm. It is like fear of the new Queen, as though they were dazzled. It is as though we were to look at the Sun itself."

Besides the rose proper, the *familia rosaceæ* includes the apples, pears, quinces, strawberries, hawthorns, medlars, cinquefoils, and *alchemilla vulgaris*, the Common Lady's Mantle.

Goethe transfigured in Dresden. Gretchen → the Mothers → the Mater Gloriosa. *Ehrfurcht*.

What is the Mystery of the Rose Cross? Why does no one speak of the White Rose Cross, the emblem of the Queen?

You remember as a child the Golden Lady watching over the City of Detroit before pollution ate into the arches and walls and turned everything to darkness. You remember.

"I trembled and my heart pounded as I ate those roses with loving relish; and no sooner had I swallowed them than I found that the promise had been no deceit. My bestial features faded away, and I became again myself, a man, Lucius, the Son of Light."

Hear us, O Lord, from heaven thy dwelling place.

The tropos of the stolen rose. *Belle et la Bette*, Tam Lin, even Eden. Eve in Eden. The trespass into the *hortus conclusus*. Once the rose is taken, the taker belongs to another. Cycles of transformation, of metamorphoses, ensue. The beloved becomes a monster, a wolf, a fire, a lion, a man. Metaphor and reality unite here, the *coniunctio poetica*, for the soul holds no constant form.

162

"The god of *zoë* was the only one of the gods who came into the world as an embryo, as a being whose first movement in the womb was the most direct manifestation of life, something which only women can experience."

Janet takes the rose and finds that she's with child. So it is with all who take a rose, a rose but only two.

You find all your love letters in a wooden box at the foot of her bed. A box of dreams, a trove sprinkled with rose petals.

You remember kissing the Beloved when she took a rose petal from your mouth into hers.

Rosa dat mel apibus.

The darkness of the cave. Three queens and fifty maidens. The children in the clouds.

"The eggs of the bee are perfectly round, and very small, being only about one-eighth of a line in diameter. In the ducts of the ovarium, they are ranged together in the form of a rosary."

You place a holy card of the Virgin on a hive's empty frame and the bees build their own frame around her and venerate her image.

Receive each other with a holy kiss.

Hear us, O Lord, from heaven thy dwelling place.

You visit the tiny Orthodox church in Fraser to see the miraculous icon of St. Phanourios. Mysterious etchings have appeared on the glass protecting the image, echo the saint's halo and the halo of the taper he holds. But you feel a stronger presence, a force, shooting as if from a reliquary near the iconostasis. You ask the priest what's in the container. A relic of the Virgin.

"*Alitur enim liquántibus ceris,*
quas in substántiam pretiósæ huius lámpadis
apis mater edúxit."

Demeter, goddess of the Earth and of grain, had for her priest-
esses the *Melissae*, the nymphs of the bees, bringers of fertility.
Demeter's beloved daughter Persephone, as feminine psychopomp, was also known as the Queen and Virgin of the Bees.
Belonging to the worlds of both the living and the dead, she
knew all secrets.

A white cloud appears over the Rose of Sharon one February,
on a day you contemplate suicide. You are bankrupt, weighed
down by your own fallenness, your wrecklessness, your fear.
Then . . . the Kiss.

For cult see *Rose*.

TO MAKE A WHITE METHEGLIN.
    Take Sweet-bryar buds, Violet-leaves, Strawberry-leaves, and
the petals of Eglantine, of each one handful, and a good handful
of Apple-flowers. Boil all these three-quarters of an hour. Then
strain it, and when it is blood-warm, put in as much of the
best honey, as will make the Liquor bear an Egg the breadth of
six pence above the water. Then boil again as long as you will
and set it abroad a-cooling. Then tun it. You may make this a
little before Michaelmas, and it will be ready to drink at Lent.

Dante's vision: the *Rosa mundi*. But you saw Jesus crucified in
a rose in 1992 in a gardened churchyard in Bloomfield Hills,
Michigan on a May morning when even darkness spoke.

The antique perfume bottle holds a cotton ball saturated in oil
from a weeping icon: after twenty-four years still fresh, pure
virgin olive oil, redolent with roses.

The Queen is born from out of the Sun, and brings Sun-light
with her own body.

A box of dreams, a trove sprinkled with rose petals.

Hear us, O Lord, from heaven thy dwelling place.

Nikolai Berdyaev

PHILOSOPHY, PROPHECY, ESCHATOLOGY

WRITING ABOUT THE PHILOSOPHY OF Nikolai Berdyaev is something of a betrayal. Indeed, his distrust of academic philosophy—a thinking, a critique *about* philosophy but not actually philosophy in deed—condemns me as his betrayer, or worse: condemns me as one who betrays Sophia, philosophy in its true being. This is not to say there are no inconsistencies in his philosophy. Every philosophy bears the weight of its own improbability. Berdyaev knew this and openly admitted it. As he writes in *Slavery and Freedom* (1939), "The inconsistencies and contradictions which are to be found in my thought are expressions of spiritual conflict, of contradictions which lie at the very heart of existence itself, and are not to be disguised by a façade of logical unity."[1] Any attempt to characterize Berdyaev's thought, protean and creative as it is, will by necessity be plagued by contingency. Nevertheless, I would like in this essay to, at the very least, inaugurate a contemplation of the role of prophecy in Berdyaev's thought. For the philosophy of Berdyaev, perhaps more than that of any other modern philosopher—even Solovyov and Shestov—dwells in the future and the realm of the eschaton. In this, his philosophical project is thoroughly and unapologetically, even defiantly, Christian.

For Berdyaev, philosophy is many things, but it is in no way an academic exercise performed for one's peers. The idea

---

1 Nikolai Berdyaev, *Slavery and Freedom*, trans. R. M. French (New York: Charles Scribner's Sons, 1944), 8.

of conformity to the opinions of even a highly cultured group repelled him, as it always compromises the essential freedom of the philosopher who sells his birthright for a plate of lentils by appealing to the crowd, however sophisticated its opinions. Berdyaev holds that philosophy is primarily a creative act, and as such it must resist the temptation of acceptance promised by professional approval. As he writes,

> The highly cultured man of a certain style usually expresses imitative opinions upon every subject: they are average opinions, they belong to a group, though it may well be that this imitativeness belongs to a cultured élite and to a highly select group. . . . Genius has never been completely able to find a place for itself in culture, and culture has always striven to turn genius from a wild animal into a domestic animal.[2]

The philosopher, as wild animal, has no proper place in the domesticated world of the academy.

Because of the wild and creative vocation of the philosopher, Berdyaev begins The Meaning of the Creative Act (1916) with a chapter entitled "Philosophy as a Creative Act." Annoyed by the tendency for some philosophers and philosophical schools to treat philosophy as a science, Berdyaev reclaims the rightful province of this art:

> Philosophy is an art rather than a science. Philosophy is a special art, differing in principle from poetry, music, or painting — it is the art of knowing. Philosophy is art because it is creation. Philosophy is art because it predicates a calling and a special gift from above, because the personality of its creator is impressed upon it, no less than on music or poetry. . . . Philosophy is the art of knowing in freedom by creating ideas which resist the given world and necessity and penetrate into the ultimate essence of the world. We cannot make art dependent

---

2   Nikolai Berdyaev, Slavery and Freedom, 123.

upon science, creativeness upon adaptation, freedom
upon necessity.[3]

As an art, then, philosophy is, like all arts, characterized by acts
of intuition, "the *sine qua non* of philosophy."[4]

As intuitive act, philosophy for Berdyaev is simultaneously
a revelatory act. Because it is a revelatory act, philosophy, as
in the Scholastic tradition and its modern iterations in Idealism and Positivism, need not be restricted in its freedom by a
claustrophobic obedience to rationality. Revelation transforms
philosophy.[5] Nevertheless, the philosopher cannot simply sur-
render to atavistic acceptance of religious claims — for then he
would no longer be a philosopher: "The philosopher's tragedy
has its origin in the attempt to restrict his pursuit of knowledge by the invocation of Divine Grace or by the appeal to the
universal character of natural necessity."[6] In his occupation of
a *metaxu* between religion and science, the philosopher finds
himself in conflict with both, yet participates in the milieux
they explore.

Nevertheless, for Berdyaev, philosophy is at its core a religious striving, a striving with ontology, a struggle with God,
despite atheistic, materialist, or rationalistic claims to the contrary. "It is quite useless for philosophy to disguise its true
nature," he writes in *Freedom and the Spirit* (1927), "for it is
always positively or negatively religious."[7] Like Pierre Hadot,
for Berdyaev philosophy is a spiritual exercise, but even more
does he emphasize its reality as spiritual *activity*: "In the creative, knowing act of philosophy there is an upsurge towards
another being, another world, daring to approach the ultimate

3 Nikolai Berdyaev, *The Meaning of the Creative Act*, trans. Donald A. Lowrie
(New York: Collier Books, 1962), 30.
4 Nikolai Berdyaev, *Solitude and Society*, trans. George Reavey (London:
Geoffrey Bles/The Centenary Press, 1947), 13.
5 Ibid.
6 Ibid., 14–15.
7 Nikolai Berdyaev, *Freedom and the Spirit*, trans. Oliver Fielding Clarke
(London: Geoffrey Bles/The Centenary Press, 1935), 3.

mystery."[8] Furthermore, intellection is itself (or should be) a creative act in search of Being, though not "simply the illumination of Being, it is the light itself in the innermost depths of Being. In fact, knowledge is immanent in Being, rather than Being in knowledge."[9] One aspect of this Being occurs in the disclosure of Sophia.

Influenced by Vladimir Solovyov and in conversation with Sergei Bulgakov and Pavel Florensky (among others), Berdyaev's Sophiology nevertheless distances itself from this stream of Russian Sophiology, which he saw as somewhat contaminated by Platonism and a conscious (or unconscious) compulsion to make Sophiology congruent with patristics and theological dogma — and therefore uncreative and unimaginative.[10] Berdyaev's Sophiology, though in many ways sympathetic to that of his compatriots, is rooted in Boehme and in theosophy, a domain in which he finds greater freedom than that to which Solovyov, Bulgakov, and Florensky confined themselves.

As a pursuit of truth and love of wisdom, philosophy is inherently sophianic for Berdyaev. The philosophic act itself indicates both a sophianic movement in the soul and points to a sophianic *telos*. "Sophia moves all true philosophy. At the summit of philosophic consciousness, Sophia enters man."[11] The sophianic, furthermore, approaches from the future and from what Berdyaev anticipates as "the new middle ages." As he writes in The End of Our Time (1924), "It is the *eternal feminine* that has so great a future in the coming history."[12] Sophia is also fundamental to Berdyaev's understanding of *transfiguration* — of society, of culture, of religion, of man, and of the earth

---

8 The Meaning of the Creative Act, 42.
9 Solitude and Society, 43.
10 Nikolai Berdyaev, The Russian Idea, trans. R. French (1947; reprt., Hudson, NY: Lindisfarne Press, 1992), 189 and 252–55. See also Mikhail Sergeev, "Sophiological Themes in the Philosophy of Nicholas Berdyaev," Transactions of the Association of Russian-American Scholars in the U. S. A. 29 (1998): 59–72.
11 The Meaning of the Creative Act, 29.
12 Nikolai Berdyaev, The End of Our Time, trans. Donald Attwater (London: Sheed & Ward, 1933), 118.

itself — so important a theme for his philosophy: "The trans-figuration of the earth is possible only through the sophianic aspect. The total denial of any sophiology leads to a deadened dualistic theism, and ultimately to deism."[13] The prophetic strain that plays so profound a part in Berdyaev's thought is unimaginable apart from his sophiology.

That prophecy as participation in the eschaton forms an integral part of Berdyaev's thought is to state the obvious. The titles of many of his books — The Fate of Russia (1918), The End of Our Time [a.k.a. The New Middle Ages] (1924), The Destiny of Man (1931), The Fate of Man in the Modern World (1934), The Beginning and the End (1947) — make this abundantly clear. As Matthew Spinka has observed, Berdyaev "is perhaps unique in his emphasis upon the creative, dynamic interpretation of eschatology."[14] That may indeed be a bit of an understatement.

Connected to his ideas on creativeness, Berdyaev's describes his attention to philosophy as revelation in terms of "active eschatology." "Active eschatology," he writes, "is the justification of the creative power in man."[15] This is so because, "The out-pouring of the Spirit, which changes the world, is the activity of the spirit in man himself."[16] Berdyaev's active eschatology, then, speaks to the regeneration of all things, or, to adopt explicitly religious terminology, their glorification. The idea of *theosis* indeed tinctures (to use Boehmian language) all of Berdyaev's thought. This glorification approaching from the future, fur-thermore, resides in the Coming of Christ which moves toward the present just as history moves toward its arrival, the two converging almost in the way of a supercollider.[17]

---

13   N. A. Berdyaev, "Studies Concerning Jacob Boehme, Etude II: The Teaching about Sophia and the Androgyne; J. Boehme and the Russian Sophiological Current" (originally appeared in Put' 21 [April 1930]: 34–62), trans. S. Janos, http://www.berdyaev.com/berdiaev/berd_lib/1930_351.html.
14   Matthew Spinka, Nicolas Berdyaev: Captive of Freedom (Philadelphia: The Westminster Press, 1950), 196.
15   Slavery and Freedom, 265.
16   Ibid.
17   Freedom and the Spirit, 304.

But the coming of the eschaton announces itself through anxiety. And while Berdyaev is assured of the final victory of Christ, he not as confident in man's willing participation in the transformations implicit in His arrival. Man, it appears, would prefer to hold onto the dead forms of the past, their shells and ghosts, than cooperate with Christ in the regeneration of all things. Certainly, something of Boehme's notion that God's love feels like terror to the sinful as it burns away the impurities of the soul haunts Berdyaev's metaphysic here. "Man is entering a new cosmos," he writes:

> All the elements of our epoch were present in the past, but now they are generalized, universalized and revealed in their true aspect. In these days of the world's agony we feel keenly that we are living in a fallen world, torn asunder by incurable contradictions. . . .
>
> The world is living in a period of agony which greatly resembles that of the end of antiquity. But the present situation is more hopeless, since at the close of antiquity Christianity entered the world as a new young force, while now Christianity, in its human age, is old and burdened with a long history in which Christians have often sinned and betrayed their ideal. And we shall see that the judgment upon history is also a judgment upon Christianity in history.[18]

Christianity, that is, in its amnesia, has forgotten how to make all things new.

But *theosis* is not the only thing that characterizes the future: there exists also what we might call a "passive eschatology," and great danger accompanies it. The defining feature of this passive eschatology has everything to do with the ways in which technology and mechanization transfigure (or, more accurately, disfigure) man as their innovations and methods are blindly and uncritically welcomed and incorporated into human life.

18   Nikolai Berdyaev, *The Fate of Man in the Modern World*, trans. Donald A. Lowrie (Ann Arbor: The University of Michigan Press, 1935), 21–22 and 23.

This movement thoroughly compromises the being of man: "We face the question, is that being to whom the future belongs to be called man, as previously, or something other?"[19] Given the subsequent colonization of the human person by genetic engineering, hormone treatments, and plastic surgery — just for starters — one would have to conclude that Berdyaev was more than prescient.

Berdyaev, like his contemporaries Martin Heidegger and Rudolf Steiner, warned about the rise of technology and its impact on human flourishing. Though he died in 1948, before the advent of television and well before the totalization of the technological and technocratic regime which has become the information revolution and the dominance of social media, his words are startlingly (and to some degree terrifyingly) poignant:

> The greatest victories of man in the realms of science, as in that of the technical mastery over nature, have become the principal cause of man's dehumanization. Man is no longer master of the machines which he has invented. Our contemporary mechanized civilization is fatal to man's inner life, for it destroys his integrity, disfigures his emotional life, makes him the instrument of inhuman processes, and takes away from him all possibility of contemplation by a rapid increase in the tempo of life.[20]

Recent warnings from repentant social media entrepreneurs Chamath Palihapitiya and Sean Parker have done nothing but affirm Berdyaev's observation, and the situation must now be far worse than he ever could have imagined. Such a dehumanized world, according to Berdyaev, "puts man under the sign of demonic possession and loss of balance."[21] As we have become all too aware, both capitalism and communism participate in this dehumanization, and no existent political structures offer an acceptable alternative. "The world threatens to become an

---

19   Ibid., 25.
20   *Towards a New Epoch*, 15.
21   *The Fate of Man in the Modern World*, 126.

organized and technicized chaos in which only the most terrible forms of idolatry and demon-worship can live."[22]

For Berdyaev, though, the rise of the technological colonization of man did not simply happen by accident. Rather, it is the result of the breakdown of culture and the failure of Christianity to transfigure society. Influenced by Solovyov's conviction that Western Christianity, while it created a culture, did not create a *Christian* culture, whereas Eastern Christianity failed to create a culture at all, (though its society was Christian),[23] Berdyaev lays the blame at the feet of a Christianity mired in its many sins and more invested in preservation of the past than concern about the future. His critique is scathing:

> We are witnessing a judgement not on history alone, but upon Christian humanity. . . . The task of creating a more just and humane social order has fallen into the hands of anti-Christians, rather than Christians themselves. The divine has been torn apart from the human. This is the basis of all judgement in the moral sphere, now being passed upon Christianity.[24]

Christianity, furthermore, failed to save culture because it failed to be Christian:

> In this visible world there is no external unity in the Church; its œcumenicity is not completely actualized. Not only the division of the Churches and the multiplicity of Christian confessions but the very fact that there are non-Christian religions in the world at all, and that there is, besides, an anti-Christian world, proves that the Church is still in a merely potential state and that its actualization is still incomplete.[25]

---

22 Ibid., 127.
23 Vladimir Solovyov, *Lectures on Divine Humanity*, trans. Peter Zouboff [1948], rev. and ed. Boris Jakim (Hudson, NY: Lindisfarne Press, 1995), 170–73.
24 *The Fate of Man in the Modern World*, 118 and 122.
25 *Freedom and the Spirit*, 348.

In addition, Christianity, for Berdyaev, is too enamored of its own past, thereby neglecting its true vocation:

> In historical Christianity the prophetic element inherent in it has become enfeebled and this is why it ceases to play an active and leading role in history. We no longer look to anything but the past and to past illumination. But it is the future which needs lighting up. [26]

And not only has the prophetic element become enfeebled, but, because it has, so has Christianity *tout court*:

> Christianity in the course of its history has too often been submissive to brute facts; the leaders of the churches have too often adapted themselves to various political and social orders, and the judgement of the Church is only pronounced after the event. The result of this has been a loss of messianic consciousness and an exclusive turning towards the past. [27]

Even the accommodationist approach to Christianity's "engagement with the world" focused on the present proves sterile: "The adapting of Christianity to the social structure and to the forces which dominated it has disfigured Christianity in the course of history and naturally provoked resentment. The spiritual depths of Christianity are no longer to be seen." [28] The picture he paints is a dire one rendered in a pallet of grey.

Faced with the realities of Christian history and culture and the impending demonic technicization of man, Berdyaev can only conclude that "Either a new epoch in Christianity is in store for us and a Christian renaissance will take place, or Christianity is doomed to perish," though he knows full well that the gates of hell shall not prevail against it. [29] Berdyaev

---

26   Nikolai Berdyaev, *Towards a New Epoch*, trans. Oliver Fielding Clarke (London: Geoffrey Bles, 1949), 36.
27   Ibid., 117.
28   Ibid., 37.
29   *Freedom and the Spirit*, 46.

wagers on behalf of the Church Triumphant, but he condemns degenerate Christianity when he sees it because he knows a failure of culture is at its core a failure of Christianity. He recognizes the paradox.

The paradox is that only Christianity can save the world from Christianity. Thus Berdyaev prophesizes the arrival of "the new Christianity" which will "rehumanize man and society, culture and the world" because "[o]nly in Divine-humanity, the Body of Christ, can man be saved."[30] But such regeneration is not without conditions:

> The future depends upon our will and upon our spiritual efforts. This must be said about the future of the entire world. The part to be played by Christianity will certainly be enormous on condition that its old fictitious forms are left behind and that its prophetic aspect is revealed as the source of a different attitude towards the social problem.[31]

In language resonant to some degree with Teilhard de Chardin's notion of the Omega Point, Berdyaev thinks of all history, of all life, as moving "towards a central even of absolute importance, the Second Coming of the Saviour."[32] Furthermore, for Berdyaev, Christianity, though it has in large part abdicated its vocation in this world, has still not completed its mission. It still has untapped reserves of creativity and revelation which lie dormant through the accretion of centuries and centuries of acquiescence to worldliness: "When there is no sense of creative mission in the Church, spiritual decadence follows."[33] Berdyaev, among other things, saw that his task was to reawaken Christianity to this mission:

> Every question has not yet been settled and Christianity is not a finished product, nor will it be finished till the

---

30 *The Fate of Man in the Modern World*, 129.
31 *Towards a New Epoch*, 117.
32 *Freedom and the Spirit*, 304.
33 Ibid., 305.

end of time; its fulfilment corresponds to the coming of the Kingdom of God. But if we are looking for this Kingdom of God and moving towards it, we cannot be in a static condition. The existence of a static Orthodoxy or Catholicism is pure fiction, a piece of mere auto-suggestion, and it arises from the objectification and "absolutization" of what are simply temporary periods in Church life.[34]

But one must wonder if in this task he failed.

The current Christian landscape suggests that, for the most part, he has. While conservative elements in Christianity (in some forms of traditionalist Catholicism, for example, certain High Church forms of Anglicanism, and throughout the Orthodox world) look to preserving an imagined past, more liberal elements of Christianity look to the present (for example, in the validation of homosexual marriage, the cultural imaginary of equity, hospitableness to LGBT people). The future, it seems, is of no one's concern. Out of sight, out of mind. For Christianity, Berdyaev would no doubt observe, this is a very real tragedy.

Complacency and the bourgeois sensibility that "one must be busy doing something" alike afflict the Christianity of which Berdyaev was so critical. Only revelation, an inherently creative movement, can remedy this. But revelation, as the stories of the prophets attest (and of which John the Baptist is perhaps the paradigmatic example), is usually unwelcome and the love it offers is interpreted as a threat: "Revelation is a catastrophic transformation of consciousness, a radical modification of its structure, almost, one might say, a creation of new organs of being with functions in another world. Revelation is not evolution but revolution."[35] It is far easier to turn away, get lost in religious nostalgia, find distraction in the politics of the moment, or engage in mindless infotainment and celebrity gossip. So stand we.

34 Ibid., 305.
35 *Freedom and the Spirit*, 96.

I cannot decide whether Berdyaev's thought is pessimistically optimistic or optimistically pessimistic. He believes in the regeneration of Christianity, of man, of culture, of nature, but sees little evidence of it in the world and even less interest. Yet he knows that, bidden or not, the Messiah comes. Like William Butler Yeats, Berdyaev is attentive to the tragic nature of revelation as it destroys the falsity of our various temptations and our bourgeois complacencies; for, "Surely some revelation is at hand; / Surely the Second Coming is at hand."[36] Berdyaev's radical Christian vision, his prophetic madness and absolute clarity, offer much to a postmodern milieu entrapped in its own excesses and excrescences. But will anyone have the time or inclination to listen?

---

36   William Butler Yeats, "The Second Coming," *The Collected Poems* (New York: Macmillan, 1933), lines 9–10.